Christmas is Coming!
Vol. 5

Compiled and Edited
by Catherine S. Corbett

Oxmoor
House®

Contents

Published by Oxmoor House, Inc., and Leisure Arts, Inc.

Library of Congress Catalog Card Number: 94-65475
ISBN: 0-8487-1441-5
ISSN: 1074-8954
Manufactured in the United States of America
First Printing

Editor-in-Chief: Nancy J. Fitzpatrick
Senior Crafts Editor: Susan Ramey Cleveland
Senior Editor, Editorial Services: Olivia Kindig Wells
Art Director: James Boone

Christmas is Coming! Vol. 5

Editor: Catherine S. Corbett
Editorial Assistant: Catherine Barnhart Pewitt
Illustrator and Designer: Barbara Ball
Copy Editor: L. Amanda Owens
Copy Assistant: Jennifer K. Mathews
Senior Photographer: John O'Hagan
Photo Stylist: Connie Formby
Production and Distribution Director: Phillip Lee
Production Manager: Gail Morris
Associate Production Manager: Theresa L. Beste
Production Assistant: Marianne Jordan
Publishing Systems Administrator: Rick Tucker

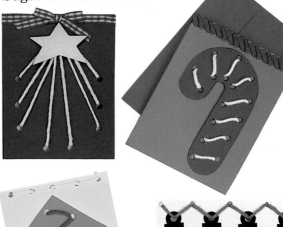

page 47

page 58

Children's Workshop: Happy Holiday Crafts

Parents' Workshop: Great Gifts for Children

page 105

3

A Note from the Editor

Listen carefully. Can you hear it? Way off in the distance the sound of Santa's sleigh bells tell us Christmas is definitely on the way!

Not long ago, when we began to plan this edition of *Christmas is Coming*, we sat down with the jolly old elf himself and asked him to share some of his thoughts and wishes for Christmas 1995. Topping Santa's wish list is his desire for boys and girls everywhere to learn the joy of giving. He said he could certainly use all the helpers he can get. We think that is a wonderful wish. In fact, we like Santa's idea so much, we decided to make it the theme of the first chapter in our book. Let me explain:

 "You Can Be Santa" is all about ways children can help others at Christmas. The chapter contains lots of projects that, one way or another, can help to make someone else's Christmas brighter.

 Several of the projects encourage a grown-up's assistance. All of the activities can be much more fun if the entire family or an entire class participates.

 Be sure to read the verses that appear at the beginning of each project. The poem will give you specific ways to use the project to help others. Some projects suggest bringing Christmas cheer to a local hospital, a charity organization, a nursing home, or an animal shelter. Be sure to contact these institutions or groups before you begin your project so that you can tailor your activity to their needs.

page 90

Getting the most from this book:

Christmas is Coming is filled with crafting fun for the whole family. There are dozens of projects for you to make. And your parents will find lots of ideas for things to make for the kids in their lives.

 The first chapter is titled "You Can Be Santa." This chapter offers projects you can make to help others have a brighter Christmas.

 "Children's Workshop" begins with "Trimmings to Fix." Here you'll find great projects to help you decorate your home or school for the holidays.

 "Presents to Make" is loaded with great gifts you can make for family and friends.

 Your mom will love "Parents' Workshop." This section begins with "Grin and Wear It," a collection of fun wearable ideas.

 "Just for Fun" is filled with toys, games, and more for grown-ups to make and give to their favorite children.

To make *Christmas is Coming* easier for you to use, we've divided the projects in "You Can Be Santa" and "Children's Workshop" into three skill levels.

Level 1 projects are very basic. Even the youngest crafters should be able to make these with a little guidance.

page 40

page 82

Level 2 projects are a little more involved and may require more time to make.

Level 3 projects are the most challenging. They may require a little help from a grown-up. They are ideal projects for older children.

When a project contains a step that should be done by or with a grown-up, we make sure to tell you in bold print.

page 16

We hope you and your parents and teachers will enjoy making the projects in this book as much as we have enjoyed putting the book together for you. So gather your crafting supplies, because *Christmas is Coming!*

Your editor,

Catharine S. Corbett

5

You Can Be Santa

**You can be Santa;
he needs helpers like you
to make Christmas better
for those who are blue.**

**So gather your friends—
making crafts is the reason—
to help those less fortunate
this holiday season.**

Cute as a Button

Deep greens and tree shapes
give the season away;
you and your friends
could make shirts in a day.

Then, wearing your sweatshirts
of buttons galore,
you can go to a nursing home
to sing carols and more.

You will need:
Purchased white sweatshirt
Waxed paper
Ruler
21 (⅞") green buttons
Fabric glue
7 (⁷⁄₁₆") yellow star buttons
9 (⁷⁄₁₆") red heart buttons
4 (⅝") green buttons

1. Place the sweatshirt faceup on a flat surface. Slide the waxed paper inside the sweatshirt. Center 1 large green button 3½" below the neckband. Referring to the photo and the drawing, make additional rows of large green buttons approximately ¼" apart, adding 1 button to each new row and spacing the buttons in each row approximately 1" apart. Glue the large green buttons in place. Let the glue dry.

2. Referring to the drawing: Center and glue 1 yellow star button above the top large green button and between the large green buttons in the third and fifth rows. Center and glue the red heart buttons between the large green buttons in the remaining rows. Let the glue dry.

3. For the tree trunk, referring to the drawing, center and glue 2 rows of the small green buttons ¼" below the last row of large green buttons, spacing the buttons in each row approximately ¼" apart. Let the glue dry. Remove the waxed paper.

Crayon Christmas Cover

A baby in the hospital
is a frail little form;
it needs a quilt to lie under
to help keep it warm.

So with some crayons that transfer,
some fabric and thread,
you can make a Christmas cover
to place in its bed.

You will need:
A grown-up
⅔ yard red minidot fabric
¼ yard green minidot fabric
Scissors
Fabric crayons
9 (10") squares each white drawing paper
   and white cotton fabric
Iron and ironing board
White thread
Sewing machine
Crib-size low-loft quilt batting
1⅓ yards Christmas miniprint fabric
   for backing
Straight pins
White pearl cotton

1. Cut 24 (3½" x 10") strips from the red minidot and 16 (3½") squares from the green minidot fabric.

2. Using the fabric crayons, draw a Christmas picture on each of the 10" squares of white paper. (Any words written will appear backwards when ironed onto the fabric, so you may want to just draw pictures.)

3. **Ask the grown-up to:** Transfer the crayon drawings to the white fabric squares, following the manufacturer's instructions.

Stitch the picture squares, the red mini-dot strips, and the green minidot squares together in strips as shown, using a ¼" seam allowance. Stitch the strips together to make the quilt top. Place the pieced quilt top on top of the batting and the backing fabric. Trim the batting and the backing to match the size of the pieced quilt top.

With the raw edges aligned, stack the backing (right side up), the pieced quilt top (right side down), and the batting; pin together. Stitch ¼" from the edges, leaving a 12" opening along 1 side for turning. Trim the corners. Turn and press. Slipstitch the opening closed.

Using the pearl cotton, take a stitch through all layers at 1 corner of 1 inside green minidot square. Tie the pearl cotton tails into a knot up against the pieced top as shown. Trim the pearl cotton tails ½" from the knot. Repeat for each corner of each inside green minidot square. Stitch only the inside corners for the squares along the edges of the quilt.

Animal Shelter Treat Totes

The holidays should be special
for God's creatures who roam,
as well as the helpers
who provide them a home.

A fun way to share
is stuffing totes that are small—
for the workers, fill with snacks;
for the pets, a toy ball.

You will need (for each tote):
A grown-up
Tracing paper
Pencil
Scissors
5" square paper-backed fusible web
Iron and ironing board
White fleece scrap
Red felt scrap
5" x 6" piece heavy cardboard
5" x 6" canvas minitote
Black fabric paint with tip
Thick craft glue
½"-diameter white pom-pom
2 (7-mm) wiggle eyes
6" length ⅛"-wide green satin ribbon
For the dog: black felt scrap, 5" square
   brown pinwale corduroy
For the cat: pink felt scrap, 5" square gray
   pinwale corduroy, 4-mm pink pom-pom

1. Trace the hat, hatband, and body patterns. Transfer them to the paper side of the fusible web. Cut them out, adding approximately ¼" outside the shapes. **For the dog,** also trace and transfer each ear and the nose. **For the cat,** also trace and transfer the inner ear.

2. Ask the grown-up to fuse the hatband shape to the white fleece scrap and the hat shape to the red felt scrap, following the manufacturer's instructions. **For the dog,** also fuse the ears and the body to the brown corduroy and the nose to the black felt. **For the cat,** also fuse the inner ear to the pink felt and the body to the gray corduroy. Cut out the shapes along the outlines.

3. Insert the piece of cardboard into the tote. **Ask the grown-up** to center and fuse the body to 1 side of the tote. Referring to the pattern for placement, fuse the remaining pieces in place.

14

4. Using the black fabric paint, outline each of the pieces. **For the dog,** also draw the mouth and the freckles. **For the cat,** also draw the mouth and the whiskers. Let the paint dry.

5. Referring to the pattern: Glue the white pom-pom in place on the hat. Glue the wiggle eyes in place. Tie the ribbon into a bow and glue it in place. **For the cat,** glue the pink pom-pom above the mouth for the nose. Let the glue dry.

Hat
Cut 1.

Attach white pom-pom here.

Inner Ear
Cut 1.

Hatband
Cut 1.

Cat Body
Cut 1.

Attach bow here.

Attach pink pom-pom here.

Attach white pom-pom here.

Hat
Cut 1.

Ear
Cut 1.

Hatband
Cut 1.

Ear
Cut 1.

Nose

Dog Body
Cut 1.

Attach bow here

15

Heavenly Host Coin-Keeper

This sweet angel bank is a great place to keep some change and some coins from the earnings you reap.

With the money you save, you could bring so much joy to a child who may otherwise not be getting a toy.

You will need:
A grown-up
Tracing paper
Pencil
Scissors
White heavyweight paper:
    2 (9½") squares, 1 (4") square
Gold paint pen
1 potato chip canister with lid
Transparent tape
Craft glue
2 (¾"-diameter) white pom-poms
Craft knife
10" length 1"-wide lace
9" length gold cording
1 gold ribbon rosette
1 screw with ¼"-diameter head
Masking tape
1 (3"-diameter) Styrofoam ball
2 (10-mm) wiggle eyes
Pink paper scrap
Fine-tip permanent black marker
1 gold tinsel pipe cleaner
9" x 72" piece white netting
White thread

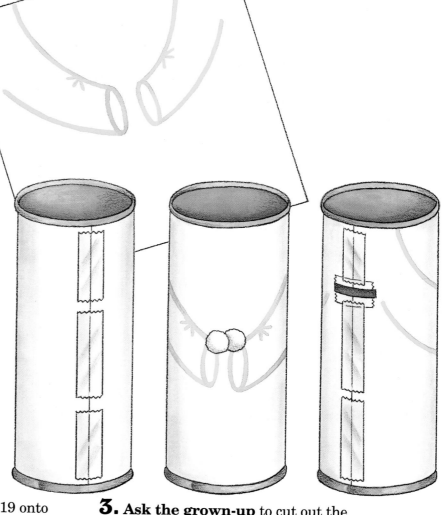

1. Trace the arms pattern on page 19 onto the tracing paper. Cut them out. Center and transfer the patterns to 1 edge of 1 (9½") square of white paper as shown. Outline the arms using the gold paint pen.

2. Wrap the remaining 9½" square of white paper around the canister. Using the transparent tape, tape the ends together where they meet in the back. Repeat to wrap and tape the square with the arms around the covered canister, with the top of the arms along the canister opening edge. Referring to the photo, glue the pom-poms in place for the hands. Let the glue dry.

3. Ask the grown-up to cut out the money slot where shown, using the craft knife. Cover the edges of the opening with the transparent tape.

4. Center the canister lid upside down on the 4" square of white paper and trace around it. Cut out the circle. Glue it to the top of the lid. Let the glue dry.

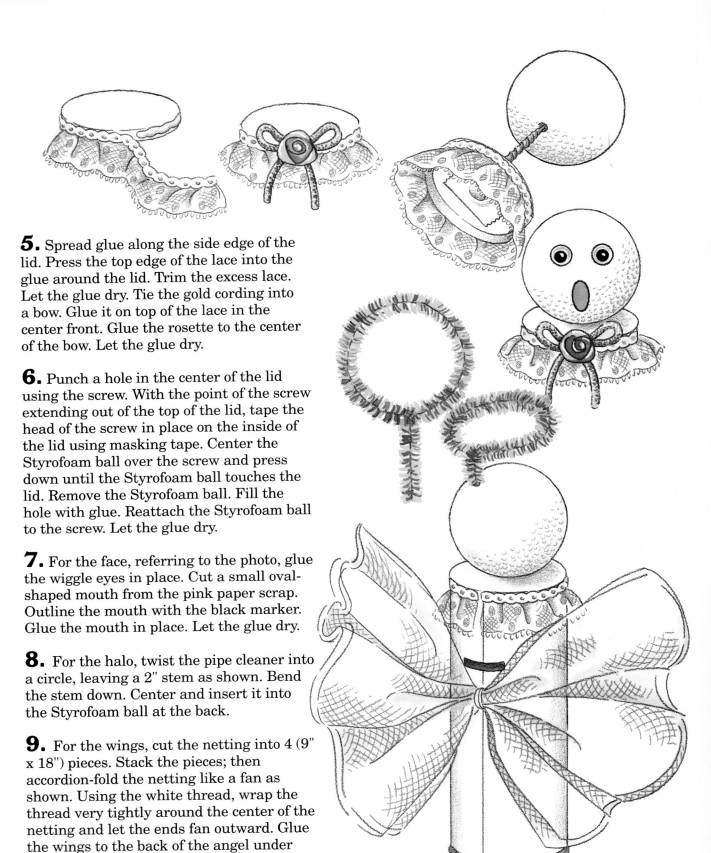

5. Spread glue along the side edge of the lid. Press the top edge of the lace into the glue around the lid. Trim the excess lace. Let the glue dry. Tie the gold cording into a bow. Glue it on top of the lace in the center front. Glue the rosette to the center of the bow. Let the glue dry.

6. Punch a hole in the center of the lid using the screw. With the point of the screw extending out of the top of the lid, tape the head of the screw in place on the inside of the lid using masking tape. Center the Styrofoam ball over the screw and press down until the Styrofoam ball touches the lid. Remove the Styrofoam ball. Fill the hole with glue. Reattach the Styrofoam ball to the screw. Let the glue dry.

7. For the face, referring to the photo, glue the wiggle eyes in place. Cut a small oval-shaped mouth from the pink paper scrap. Outline the mouth with the black marker. Glue the mouth in place. Let the glue dry.

8. For the halo, twist the pipe cleaner into a circle, leaving a 2" stem as shown. Bend the stem down. Center and insert it into the Styrofoam ball at the back.

9. For the wings, cut the netting into 4 (9" x 18") pieces. Stack the pieces; then accordion-fold the netting like a fan as shown. Using the white thread, wrap the thread very tightly around the center of the netting and let the ends fan outward. Glue the wings to the back of the angel under the slot. Let the glue dry.

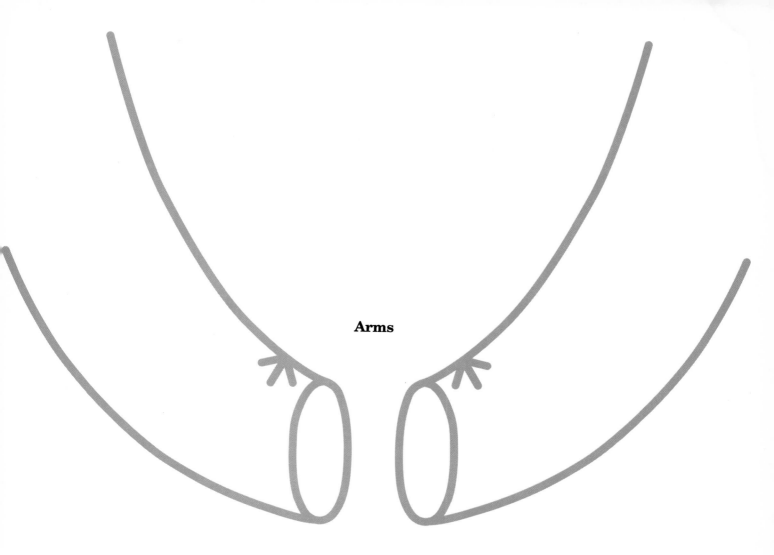

Arms

Greetings from the USA

Christmas may be lonely
for soldiers overseas;
a fun holiday greeting
is a sure way to please.

A card with a message
so warm and so true
lets them know they're appreciated
for all that they do.

You will need (for each card):
Tracing paper
Pencil
Scissors
Ruler
Craft glue
For the stocking: 8" x 10" piece red heavyweight paper, white and blue heavyweight paper scraps
For the flag: 9" x 12" piece white heavyweight paper, 1 sheet white typing paper, blue and red construction paper scraps

1. For the stocking: Trace the stocking, cuff, heel, toe, and star patterns on page 23 onto the tracing paper. Cut them out.

2. Fold the red paper in half, short ends together. Place the stocking pattern on the folded paper, aligning the heel edge of the stocking with the folded edge of the paper. Transfer the stocking onto the paper. Remove the pattern and cut out the stocking. Do not cut the side fold; it will become the hinged side of the card.

3. Using the pencil and the ruler, draw 4 approximately ⅜" x 7" strips and 2 approximately ⅜" x 3" strips onto the white paper. Cut them out. (The strips do not have to be cut evenly.) Transfer the cuff, heel, and toe patterns onto the remaining white paper. Cut them out. Referring to the pattern and the drawing, glue the pieces in place on the front of the stocking, beginning with the strips. Transfer 12 stars onto the blue paper. Cut them out. Glue 6 stars to the cuff, 4 stars to the heel, and 2 stars to the toe. Let the glue dry.

21

4. For the flag: Fold the white heavy-weight paper in half, short ends together. The fold will become the hinged top of the card.

5. Using the pencil and the ruler, draw a 4" square onto the blue paper. Cut it out. Glue the square in the top left corner of the front of the card.

6. Tear 3 approximately ¾" x 5" strips and 1 approximately ¾" x 9" strip from the red paper. Referring to the pattern and the drawing, glue them in place.

7. To make the snowflake, cut a 4" square from the typing paper. Fold the paper as shown. Cut notches in the folded edges. Unfold the snowflake and finger-press it flat. Center and glue the snowflake on the blue square.

22

To send your greeting to a soldier stationed away from home, either here in the United States or in a foreign country, please follow these guidelines:

1. Place your card in an envelope and write your return address in the upper left corner of the envelope. Write "Mail For Our Military" across the center of the envelope.

2. *Paperclip* a first class postage stamp to the envelope.

3. Place the envelope containing your card into a larger envelope. Address the larger envelope to:

Mail For Our Military
P.O. Box 339
Soldier, KY 41173

Sweet-Smelling Ornaments

For your neighbor who's elderly
and not able to decorate,
take her a tree—
the whole family can participate.

Make ornaments of cinnamon
and add a skirt around the base;
she'll love the spice scent
as it adds color to her place.

**You will need (for 12 approximately
2½"-wide ornaments):**
2 (1.9 ounce) bottles ground cinnamon
Large mixing bowl
½ to ¾ cup applesauce
Rolling pin
Waxed paper
Cookie cutters in desired shapes
Cookie sheet
1 plastic drinking straw
¼"-wide satin ribbon in desired colors
Scissors

1. Pour the cinnamon into the large mixing
bowl, reserving a small amount to use later.
Add the applesauce a little at a time, mixing
with your hands until a stiff dough forms.

2. Coat the rolling pin with the reserved
cinnamon. Place the dough on the waxed
paper. Roll out the dough to a ¼" thickness.
Using the cookie cutters, cut out the
ornaments. Place the ornaments on the
cookie sheet. Using 1 end of the straw,
make a hole in the top of each ornament.

3. Let the ornaments dry on the cookie
sheet for several days, turning them over
occasionally.

4. Cut 1 (16") length of ribbon for each
ornament. For the hangers, thread a 16"
length of ribbon through each hole. Tie the
ends of each length into a bow.

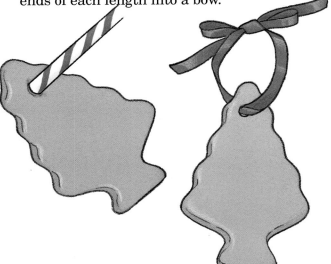

Joy Banner

WORLD
BANNER
BOOTH

Let's not forget the planet,
because it needs us as well;
perhaps you can raise money
with some banners to sell.

You can give the earned funds
to groups supporting the Earth,
those who understand its value
and know what it's worth.

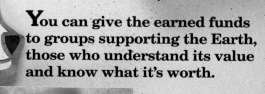

FOR
SALE
NOW

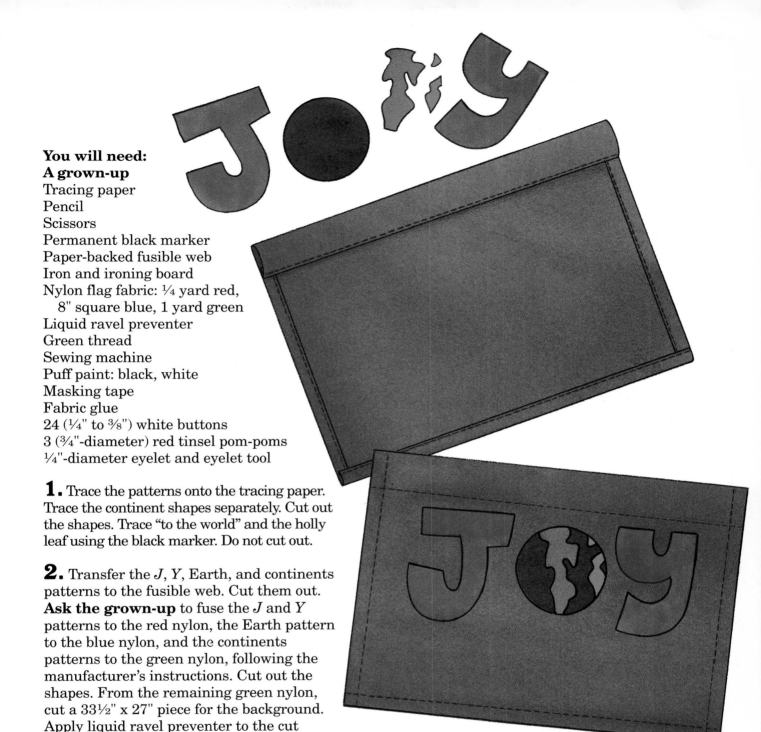

You will need:
A grown-up
Tracing paper
Pencil
Scissors
Permanent black marker
Paper-backed fusible web
Iron and ironing board
Nylon flag fabric: ¼ yard red,
   8" square blue, 1 yard green
Liquid ravel preventer
Green thread
Sewing machine
Puff paint: black, white
Masking tape
Fabric glue
24 (¼" to ⅜") white buttons
3 (¾"-diameter) red tinsel pom-poms
¼"-diameter eyelet and eyelet tool

1. Trace the patterns onto the tracing paper. Trace the continent shapes separately. Cut out the shapes. Trace "to the world" and the holly leaf using the black marker. Do not cut out.

2. Transfer the *J*, *Y*, Earth, and continents patterns to the fusible web. Cut them out. **Ask the grown-up** to fuse the *J* and *Y* patterns to the red nylon, the Earth pattern to the blue nylon, and the continents patterns to the green nylon, following the manufacturer's instructions. Cut out the shapes. From the remaining green nylon, cut a 33½" x 27" piece for the background. Apply liquid ravel preventer to the cut edges of the nylon pieces. Let them dry.

3. Ask the grown-up to hem the sides and the bottom of the background by folding the short edges and 1 long edge under ¼" and then 1"; press. Stitch close to the first fold. For the casing, fold the remaining raw edge under ¼" and then 3¼"; press. Stitch close to the first fold.

4. Ask the grown-up to fuse the *J* and the *Y* to the background, each 4½" from 1 side edge and 4¾" from the top. Fuse the continent shapes in place on the Earth piece. Then center and fuse the Earth between the *J* and the *Y*.

Level 3

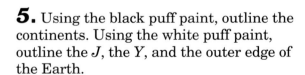

5. Using the black puff paint, outline the continents. Using the white puff paint, outline the *J*, the *Y*, and the outer edge of the Earth.

6. To transfer "to the world" and the holly leaf to the banner, use the masking tape to tape the pattern to a window. Position the banner faceup on top so that the pattern is 6" from each side of the banner and 4½" from the bottom edge. Tape the banner to the window. Using the pencil, transfer the letters and the holly leaf. Remove the banner and the pattern from the window.

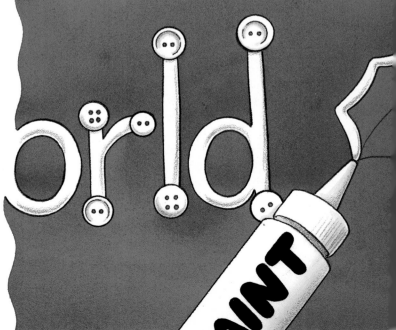

7. Using the white puff paint, fill in the letters and outline the holly leaf. Let the paint dry. Referring to the photo, glue the buttons in place on the letters; glue the pom-poms at the bottom tip of the holly leaf.

8. Place the banner facedown on a flat surface. In the top left corner, mark the center of the 1" hem. **Ask the grown-up** to hammer the eyelet in place, using the eyelet tool and following the manufacturer's instructions. When flying the banner, thread the flagpole lacings through the eyelet to hold the banner in place.

Check the Social Sciences reference section of your local library for these books to learn more about the various environmental organizations you may wish to support.

Your Resource Guide to Environmental Organizations. Edited by John Seredich. Irvine, CA: Smiling Dolphins Press, 1991.

Lanier-Graham, Susan D. *The Nature Directory: A Guide to Environmental Organizations.* New York: Walker Publishing Company, Inc., 1991.

30

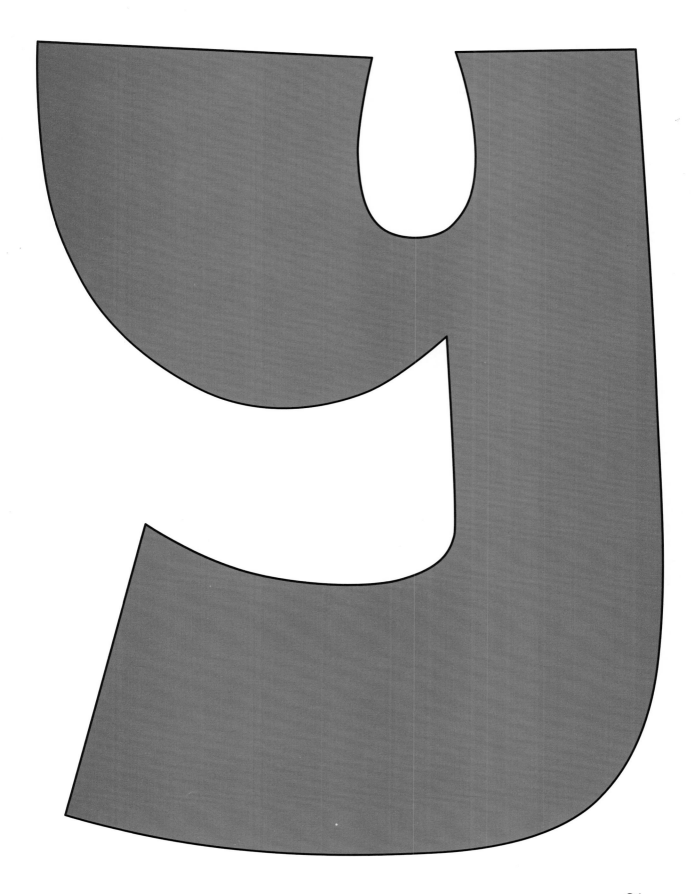

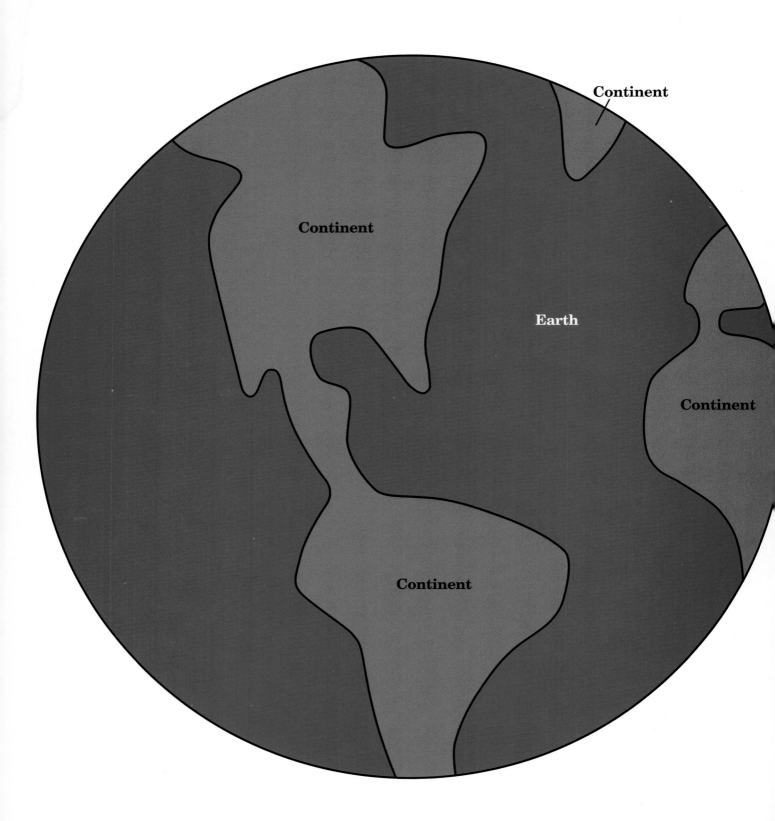

Continent

Continent

Earth

Continent

Continent

Sugar-Sweet Snowman

Make a few special treats
to brighten a hospital stay,
for those who would rather
be home on Christmas Day.

A candy-filled snowman
is a very nice way
to enliven a dull,
old hospital tray.

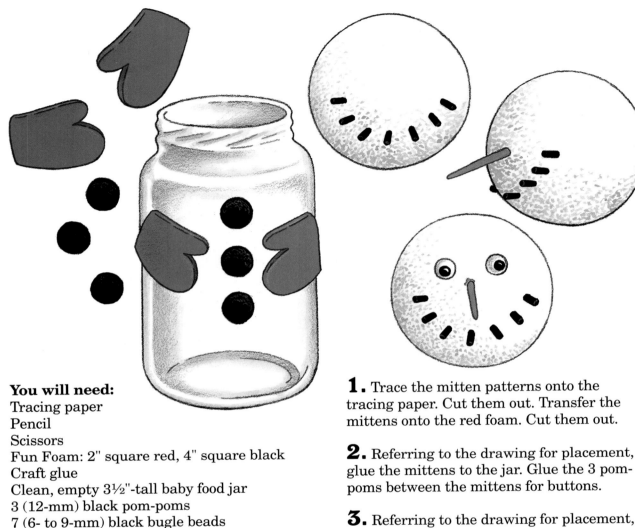

You will need:
Tracing paper
Pencil
Scissors
Fun Foam: 2" square red, 4" square black
Craft glue
Clean, empty 3½"-tall baby food jar
3 (12-mm) black pom-poms
7 (6- to 9-mm) black bugle beads
2"-diameter Styrofoam ball
Toothpick
Orange permanent marker
2 (7-mm) wiggle eyes
Dinner knife
1½"-diameter black spool
Wooden craft stick
14" length ¼"-wide red grosgrain ribbon
   with black dots
Peppermint candies

Note: If you cannot locate a black spool,
use black spray paint to paint a white
spool. Let the paint dry thoroughly.

1. Trace the mitten patterns onto the
tracing paper. Cut them out. Transfer the
mittens onto the red foam. Cut them out.

2. Referring to the drawing for placement,
glue the mittens to the jar. Glue the 3 pom-
poms between the mittens for buttons.

3. Referring to the drawing for placement,
make the snowman's mouth by inserting
the bugle beads halfway into the Styrofoam
ball. To secure the beads, remove them 1 at
a time from the Styrofoam ball, dip 1 end in
the glue, and then reinsert the glue end
into the Styrofoam ball. Let the glue dry.

4. Break the toothpick so that it measures
approximately 1" long. Use the orange
marker to color the 1" length. Referring to
the drawing for placement, insert the toothpick into the Styrofoam ball. Remove it and
dip the broken end into the glue; then
reinsert the glue end into the Styrofoam
ball for the nose. Glue the wiggle eyes
above the nose. Let the glue dry.

5. Cut 1 (2½"-diameter) circle and 1 (1½"-diameter) circle from the black foam. Using the dinner knife, saw off the top of the Styrofoam ball to create a flat base on which to place the hat. Glue the 2½"-diameter circle to the top flat part. Center and glue 1 end of the spool on the 2½"-diameter circle. Center and glue the remaining circle on the top of the spool. Let the glue dry.

6. Break the craft stick so that it measures approximately 3" long. Insert the broken end approximately 1" into the bottom of the Styrofoam ball. (The stick will help keep the snowman's head on the jar.) To secure the stick, remove it from the ball, dip 1 end in the glue, and then reinsert the glue end of the stick into the ball. Let the glue dry.

7. For the scarf, knot the ribbon around the rim of the jar. Fill the jar with peppermints. Fit the head in the top of the jar, inserting the stick between the candies.

35

Once the crafts are all finished,
and you've helped do your part,
you'll feel happy inside,
and all warm in your heart.

And as you lay down your head
on Christmas Eve night,
you'll know Santa is pleased
you've helped make Christmas
    so bright!

Children's Workshop
Happy Holiday Crafts

Trinket Top Cookie Jar

Tiny ornaments, miniature lights, and sequin stars fill the lid of a glass jar to create a unique Christmas container. Fill the jar with cookies for a holiday hostess gift.

You will need:
A grown-up
Glass jar with rubber-stopped hollow lid
Assorted tiny Christmas decorations
24" length grosgrain ribbon

1. Remove the lid from the jar. Remove the rubber stopper from the lid. (You may need to **ask a grown-up** to help you.)

2. Fill the lid with the decorations. Replace the rubber stopper.

3. Replace the lid on the jar. Tie the ribbon into a bow around the mouth of the jar.

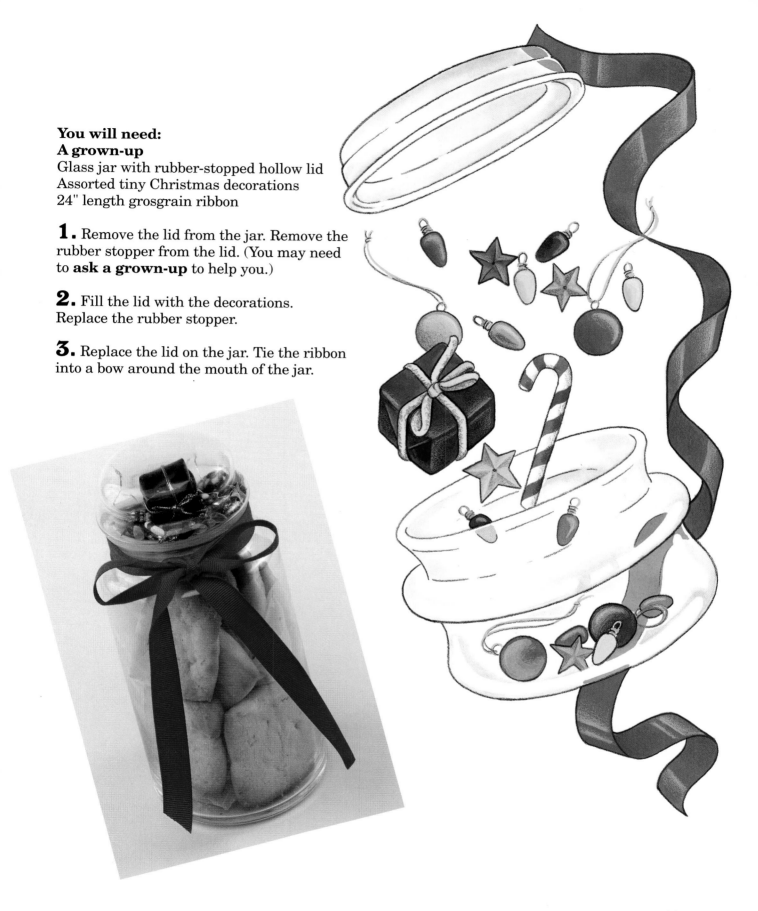

41

Treasures from Trash

Don't throw away those old drawings or greeting cards—recycle them and make paper ornaments or package toppers. Choose cookie cutters in unique shapes and create decorations that are environmentally friendly.

You will need (for each ornament):
A grown-up
1 sheet used construction paper or 1
    greeting card
Electric blender
2 cups warm water
Window screen
Cookie cutter in desired shape
Ribbon scrap
Thick glue
Assorted trinkets, curling ribbon, or
    costume jewels

1. Remove staples, tape, or other nonpaper items from the paper. Tear the paper into tiny pieces and place them in the blender.

2. Ask the grown-up to watch as you do this step: Pour the warm water into the blender. Place the lid on the blender and process the mixture until it becomes a thick pulp.

3. Place the window screen over a sink. Place the cookie cutter on top of the screen and fill it with the paper mixture. Let the water drain completely. Carefully remove the cookie cutter and let the ornament air dry overnight.

4. To make the hanger, fold the ribbon in half and glue the ends to the back of the ornament at the center top. Decorate the ornament as desired with the trinkets, the curling ribbon, or the jewels.

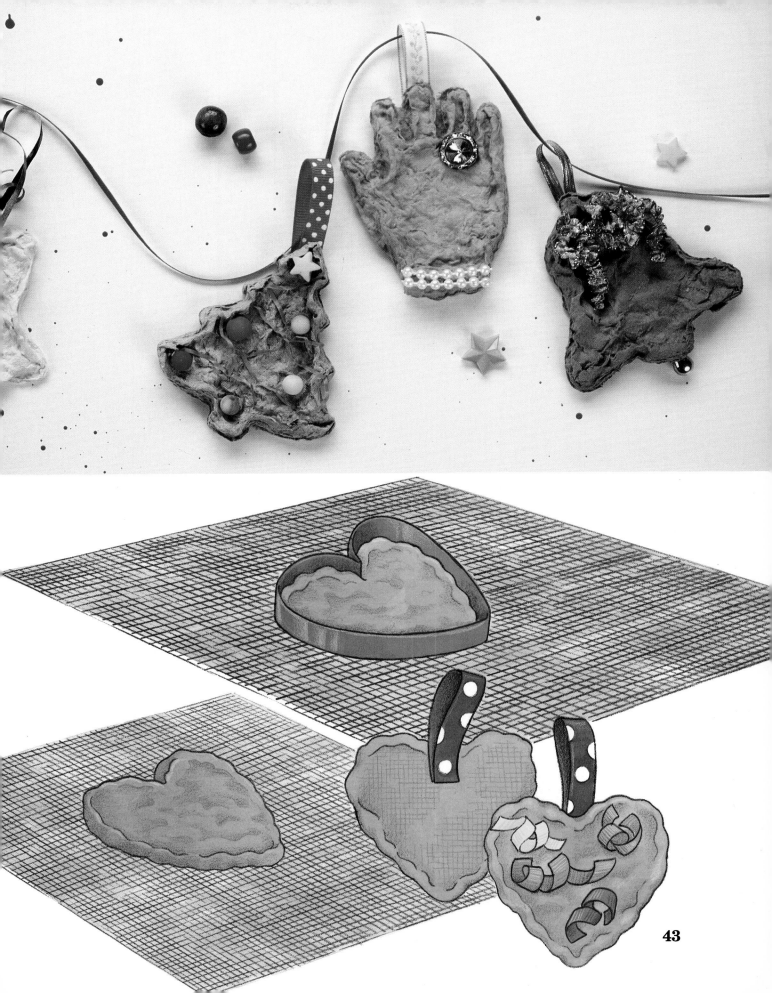

Merry Mobile

Whether dangling from the light over the kitchen table or swinging from the ceiling fan in your room, this tree will add all the cheer of a real evergreen.

You will need:
Tracing paper
Pencil
Scissors
Fun Foam: 1 (12" x 18") sheet green; 6" square each red, blue, and white; yellow and orange scraps
Thick craft glue
6⅝ yards ⅛"-wide yellow satin ribbon

1. Trace the patterns on page 46 onto the tracing paper, transferring the markings. Cut them out.

2. Transfer 4 tree patterns onto the green foam, 1 small and 2 large package patterns onto the red foam, 1 small and 1 large package patterns onto the blue foam, and 1 small and 2 large package patterns onto the white foam. Cut them out. Then cut out 50 small circles from red, blue, white, yellow, and orange foam scraps.

3. Spread glue in the center of 1 tree. With the edges aligned, stack another tree on top. Repeat with the remaining 2 trees. Let the glue dry.

4. Cut a ⅛"-wide slit from the top of 1 joined tree shape to the midpoint indicated on the pattern. Cut a ⅛"-wide slit from the bottom center of the remaining joined tree shape to the midpoint indicated on the pattern.

5. Glue the circle ornaments randomly on the front and the back of each tree shape, being careful not to glue any circles close to the center line. Let the glue dry.

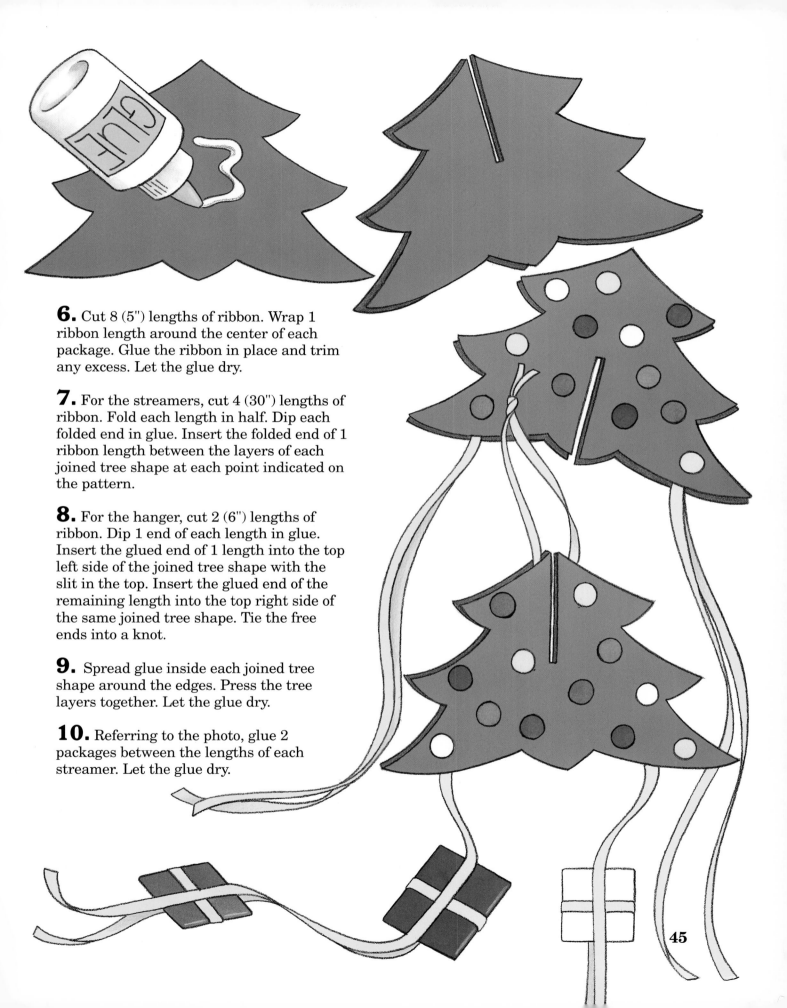

6. Cut 8 (5") lengths of ribbon. Wrap 1 ribbon length around the center of each package. Glue the ribbon in place and trim any excess. Let the glue dry.

7. For the streamers, cut 4 (30") lengths of ribbon. Fold each length in half. Dip each folded end in glue. Insert the folded end of 1 ribbon length between the layers of each joined tree shape at each point indicated on the pattern.

8. For the hanger, cut 2 (6") lengths of ribbon. Dip 1 end of each length in glue. Insert the glued end of 1 length into the top left side of the joined tree shape with the slit in the top. Insert the glued end of the remaining length into the top right side of the same joined tree shape. Tie the free ends into a knot.

9. Spread glue inside each joined tree shape around the edges. Press the tree layers together. Let the glue dry.

10. Referring to the photo, glue 2 packages between the lengths of each streamer. Let the glue dry.

45

11. Cut 8 (8") lengths of ribbon. Tie 1 length of ribbon into a bow above each package.

12. Slip the tree with the slit in the bottom onto the tree with the slit in the top.

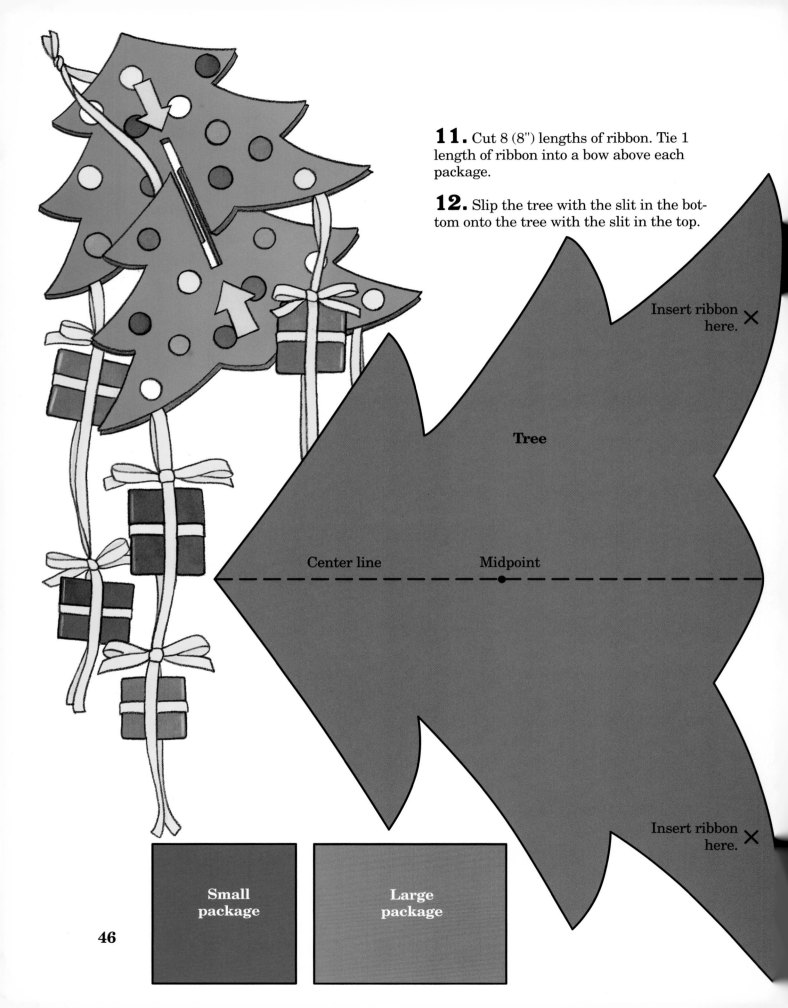

Insert ribbon here. ✕

Tree

Center line | Midpoint

Insert ribbon here. ✕

Small package

Large package

Stitching You a Merry Christmas

With just a glance at one of these cheery stitched greetings, those on your Christmas list will know that they have just received a special delivery.

You will need (for each card):
1 sheet typing paper
Scissors
Craft glue
Pencil
¼"-diameter hole punch
Plastic yarn darning needle
Transparent tape

For the Christmas tree card: 2 (4½" x 6") scraps yellow posterboard, 5" x 6" scrap green posterboard, 30" length red yarn, 20" length yellow yarn

For the star card: 2 (4½" x 6") scraps blue posterboard, 2" x 3" scrap yellow posterboard, 64" length yellow yarn, stapler, 19½" length ⅜"-wide blue plaid ribbon

For the candy cane card: 2 (4½" x 6") scraps green posterboard, 4" x 6" scrap red posterboard, 30" length white yarn, stapler, 9½" length each red and green rickrack

For the Christmas lights card: 2 (4½" x 6") scraps white posterboard; 3" square black posterboard; 2" square each red, yellow, green, and blue posterboard; 30" length green yarn

Christmas Tree Card

1. From the typing paper, cut 1 (4¼" x 5¾") piece for the inside sheet and 1 (4½" x 6") piece for the pattern tracing sheet.

2. With the edges aligned along 1 short edge, center the inside sheet vertically on 1 (4½" x 6") scrap yellow posterboard. Glue the inside sheet to the posterboard. This is the card back.

3. Trace the tree pattern on page 52 onto the tracing sheet. Using the hole punch, punch holes in the pattern where indicated. Cut out the pattern. Transfer the pattern to the 5" x 6" green posterboard scrap, marking the holes placement. Punch holes in the green posterboard at the marks. Cut out the shape.

4. Punch holes in 1 short edge of each yellow posterboard scrap where indicated. Fold the plain yellow scrap along the fold line indicated on the pattern.

5. Thread the needle with the red yarn. Tape the bottom end of the yarn to 1 side of the tree at hole #1. This is the back of the tree. Referring to the pattern, stitch in the following order, keeping the yarn taut as you sew: up in #1, down in #2; up in #3, down in #4; up in #5, down in #6; up in #5, down in #4; up in #3, down in #2. Trim the yarn and tape the end to the back of the tree at hole #2.

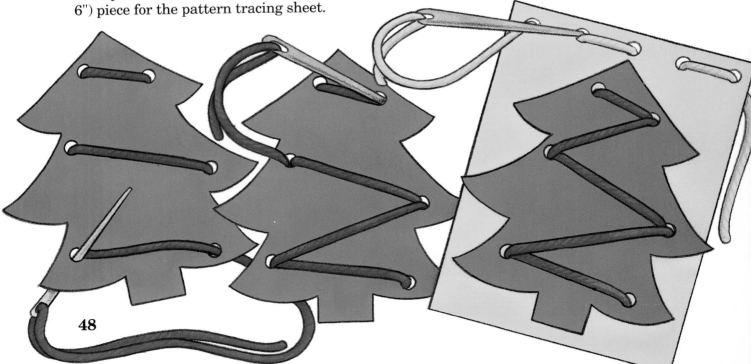

48

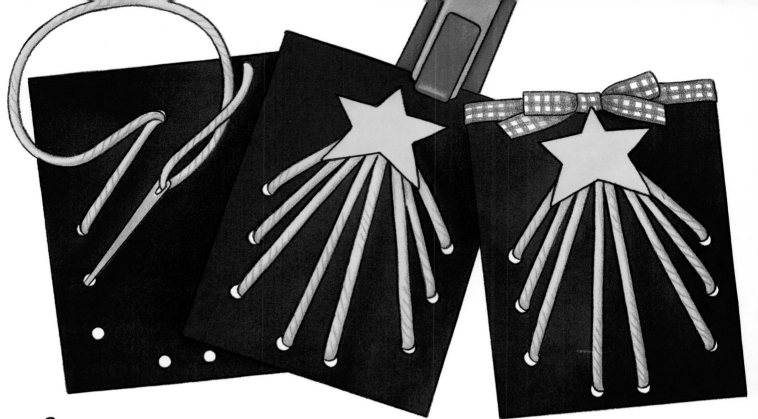

6. Glue the tree faceup to the folded yellow piece just below the fold line. Let the glue dry. (You may need to place several books on top of the tree to keep it flat.)

7. Place the card front faceup on the card back, with the top holes aligned and the inside sheet between the 2 card pieces. Thread the needle with the yellow yarn. Beginning in the far right hole and leaving a 4" tail, stitch up and down along the row of holes. When you reach the last hole, stitch back in the opposite direction through the holes. When you reach the end, tie the yarn ends together in a knot. Tape the knot to the back of the card back. Trim the excess yarn.

Star Card

1. Complete steps 1 and 2 of the Christmas Tree Card using a blue 4½" x 6" posterboard scrap. Using the hole punch, punch holes in the remaining blue posterboard scrap where indicated on the pattern. Fold the same scrap along the fold line indicated on the pattern. This is the card front.

2. Trace the star pattern on page 52 onto the tracing sheet. Cut out the pattern. Transfer the pattern to the 2" x 3" yellow posterboard scrap. Cut out the shape.

3. Thread the needle with the yellow yarn. Tape the bottom end of the yarn to 1 side of the card front at hole #1. Referring to the pattern, stitch in the following order, keeping the yarn taut as you sew: up in #1, down in #2; up in #1, down in #3; up in #1, down in #4; continue in this manner to stitch in holes #5 through #9. Trim the yarn end and tape the end to the back of the card front at hole #9.

4. Glue the top point of the star on top of hole #1. Place the card front faceup on the card back, with the inside sheet between the 2 card pieces. Staple the cards together along the top edge. Cut a 9½" length of blue plaid ribbon. Wrap the ribbon length around the top of the card, covering the staples, and overlap the ends in the back. Glue the ribbon in place. Tie the remaining ribbon into a bow. Glue the bow to the center front of the card above the top point of the star.

Candy Cane Card

1. Complete steps 1 and 2 of the Christmas Tree Card, using a 4½" x 6" green posterboard scrap. Fold the remaining green scrap along the fold line indicated on the pattern. This is the card front.

2. Trace the candy cane pattern on page 53 onto the tracing sheet. Using the hole punch, punch holes in the pattern where indicated. Cut out the pattern. Transfer the pattern to the 4" x 6" red posterboard scrap, marking the holes placement. Punch holes in the red posterboard at the marks. Cut out the shape.

3. Thread the needle with the white yarn. Tape the bottom end of the yarn to 1 side of the candy cane shape at hole #1. This is the back of the candy cane. Referring to the pattern, stitch in the following order, keeping the yarn taut as you sew: up in #1, down in #2; up in #3, down in #4; continue in this manner, ending up in #15 and down in #16. Trim the yarn end and tape the end to the back of the candy cane at hole #16.

4. Glue the candy cane faceup to the folded green posterboard piece just below the fold line. Let the glue dry. (You may need to place several books on top of the candy cane to keep it flat.)

5. Place the card front faceup on the card back, with the inside sheet between the 2 card pieces. Staple the cards together along the top edge. Interlock the 2 lengths of rickrack as shown in the photo. Wrap the rickrack around the top of the card, covering the staples, and overlap the ends in the back. Glue the rickrack in place.

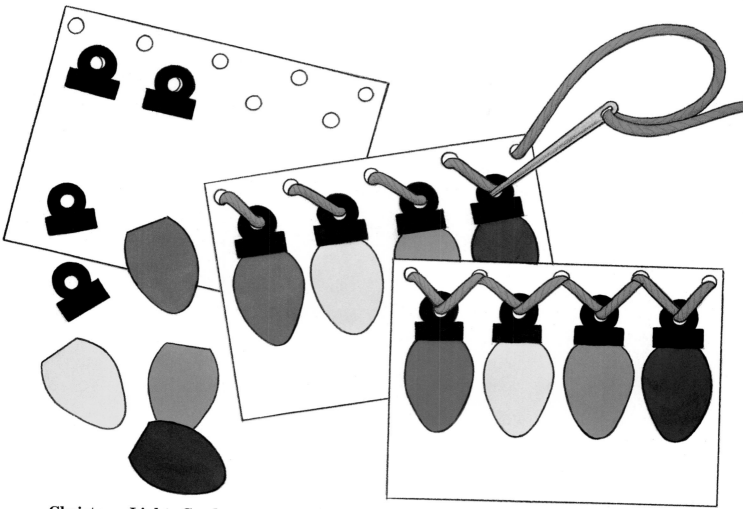

Christmas Lights Card

1. Complete steps 1 and 2 of the Christmas Tree Card, using a 4½" x 6" white posterboard scrap. Trace the light bulb and top piece patterns on page 53 onto the tracing sheet. Using the hole punch, punch a hole in the top piece pattern where indicated. Cut out the patterns. Transfer the top piece pattern 4 times to the 3" square of black posterboard, marking each hole placement. Punch holes in the top pieces at the marks. Transfer the light bulb pattern once each to the red, yellow, green, and blue posterboard squares. Cut out the shapes.

2. Punch holes in 1 long edge of each white posterboard scrap where indicated on the pattern. Fold the plain white scrap along the fold line indicated on the pattern. This is the card front.

3. Glue the top pieces to the card front so that the top piece holes align with holes #2, #4, #6, and #8 on the card front. Glue 1 light bulb beneath each top piece.

4. Place the card front faceup on the card back, with the top holes aligned and the inside sheet between the 2 card pieces. Thread the needle with the green yarn. Referring to the pattern, stitch in the following order, keeping the yarn taut as you sew: up in #1, leaving a 4" tail, down in #2; up in #3, down in #4; up in #5, down in #6; up in #7, down in #8; up in #9, down in #8; up in #7, down in #6; up in #5, down in #4; up in #3, down in #2. After the final stitch through hole #2, tie the yarn ends together in a knot. Tape the knot to the back of the card back. Trim the excess yarn.

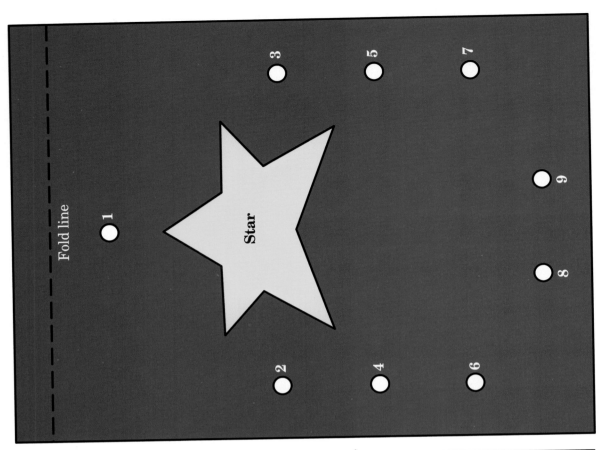

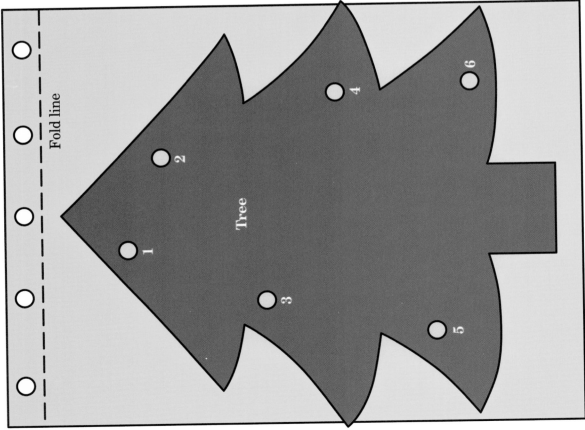

52

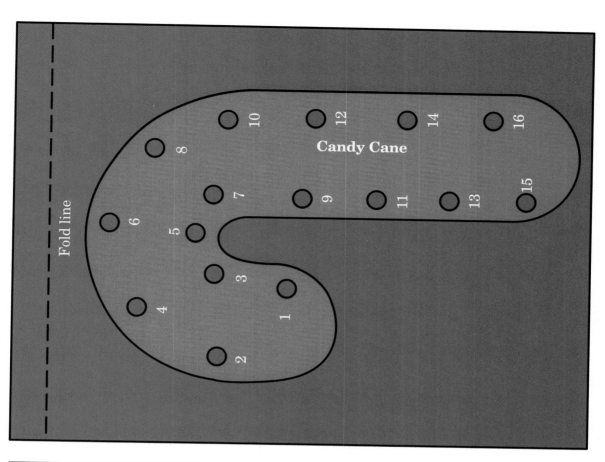

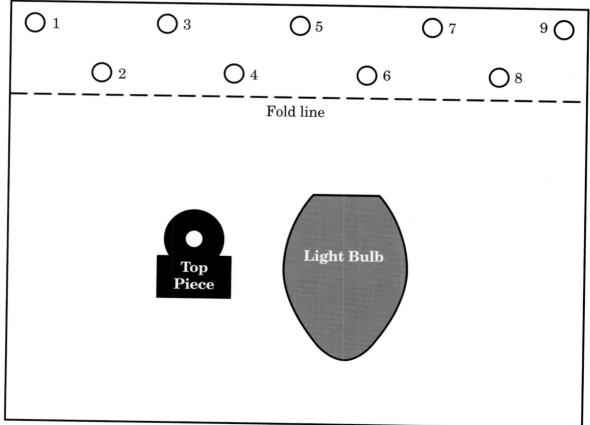

53

Nursery Rhyme Ornaments

Dreams of sailing a little boat out to sea by the light of the moon come alive with these cardboard ornaments. They look like they just popped out of a fantasy story!

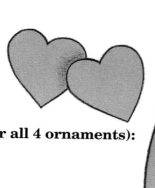

You will need (for all 4 ornaments):
Tracing paper
Pencil
Scissors
8½" x 11" piece lightweight cardboard
Permanent markers: red, black
Glue stick
Red satin ribbon: 2⅜ yards ¼"-wide,
    8" length ⅛"-wide
2 (⅛") black shank buttons
¼"-diameter hole punch
White paint pen
Embroidery scissors

1. Trace the patterns on page 57 onto the tracing paper, transferring markings. Cut them out.

2. Transfer 2 anchor patterns onto the cardboard. Transfer 1 moon pattern onto the cardboard. Reverse the moon pattern and transfer it onto the cardboard again. Transfer 2 hatbands and 2 heart cheeks to the cardboard. Cut them out.

3. For the red ribbon moon: Using the red marker, outline 1 moon, 1 heart cheek, and 1 hatband on 1 side. Referring to the drawing, cut 5 lengths from the ¼"-wide ribbon and glue them diagonally inside the hatband area. Trim the ribbon ends even with the cardboard edges. Glue the hatband in place on the moon.

4. Referring to the drawing, cut 3 lengths from the ¼"-wide ribbon and glue them across the heart cheek. Trim the ribbon ends even with the cardboard edges. Glue the heart in place on the moon.

5. Cut a 2" length from the ⅛"-wide ribbon. Glue it in place on the moon for the mouth. Trim the ribbon end even with the cardboard edge.

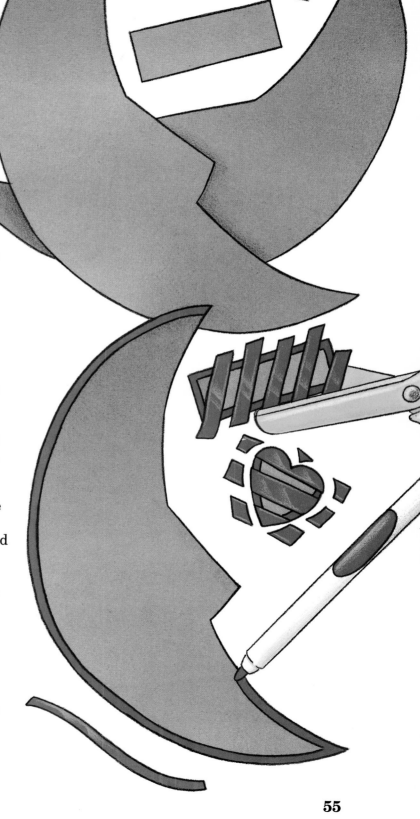

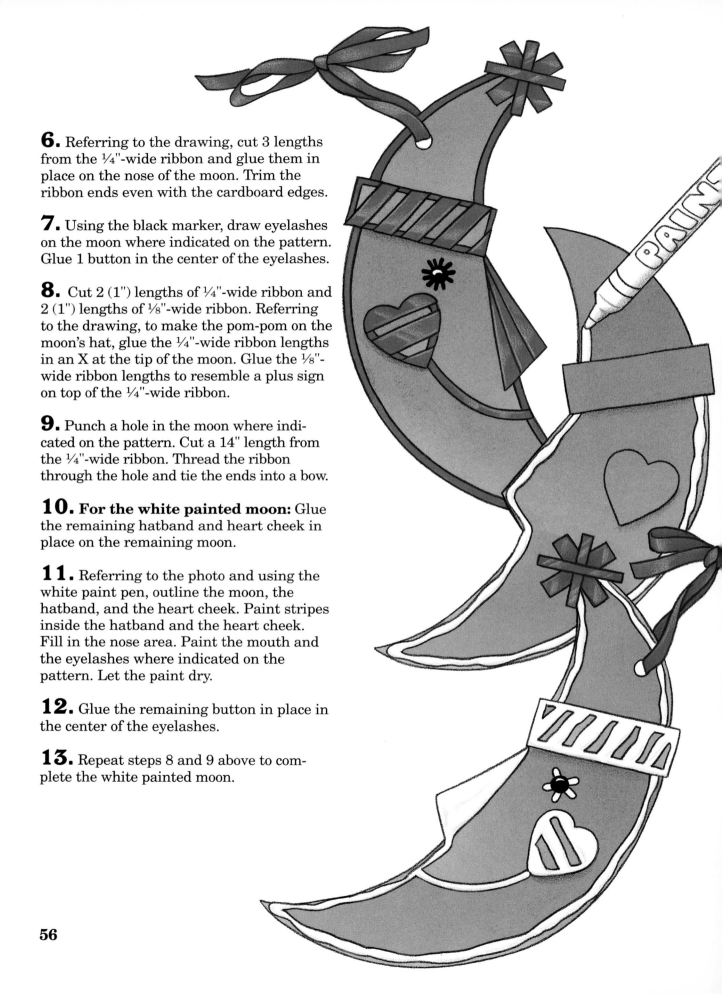

6. Referring to the drawing, cut 3 lengths from the ¼"-wide ribbon and glue them in place on the nose of the moon. Trim the ribbon ends even with the cardboard edges.

7. Using the black marker, draw eyelashes on the moon where indicated on the pattern. Glue 1 button in the center of the eyelashes.

8. Cut 2 (1") lengths of ¼"-wide ribbon and 2 (1") lengths of ⅛"-wide ribbon. Referring to the drawing, to make the pom-pom on the moon's hat, glue the ¼"-wide ribbon lengths in an X at the tip of the moon. Glue the ⅛"-wide ribbon lengths to resemble a plus sign on top of the ¼"-wide ribbon.

9. Punch a hole in the moon where indicated on the pattern. Cut a 14" length from the ¼"-wide ribbon. Thread the ribbon through the hole and tie the ends into a bow.

10. For the white painted moon: Glue the remaining hatband and heart cheek in place on the remaining moon.

11. Referring to the photo and using the white paint pen, outline the moon, the hatband, and the heart cheek. Paint stripes inside the hatband and the heart cheek. Fill in the nose area. Paint the mouth and the eyelashes where indicated on the pattern. Let the paint dry.

12. Glue the remaining button in place in the center of the eyelashes.

13. Repeat steps 8 and 9 above to complete the white painted moon.

14. **For the red ribbon anchor:** Using the embroidery scissors, cut out the heart-shaped ribbon hole from 1 cardboard anchor, being careful not to cut into it from an outside edge. Using the red marker, outline the anchor and the hole on 1 side. Referring to the photo, cut 3 lengths from the ¼"-wide ribbon and glue them diagonally along the center part of the anchor. Trim the ribbon ends even with the cardboard edges. Cut a 14" length from the ¼"-wide ribbon. Thread the ribbon through the hole and tie the ends into a bow.

15. **For the white painted anchor:** Using the embroidery scissors, cut out the heart-shaped ribbon hole from the remaining anchor, being careful not to cut into it from an outside edge. Using the white paint pen, outline the anchor and the hole on 1 side. Let the paint dry. Cut a 14" length from the ¼"-wide ribbon. Thread the ribbon through the hole and tie the ends into a bow.

Moon

Anchor

Sugarplum Trees

These topiaries will brighten up any tabletop or desk. We used candy circles, but many candies would work.

You will need (for 2 topiaries):
A grown-up
2 (4"-diameter) clay pots
2 (12") lengths $5/16$"-diameter wooden dowels
Acrylic paints: white, red, green, blue, yellow
Paintbrushes
Spray varnish
Tracing paper
Pencil
Scissors
10" square cardboard
Craft knife
Paper plate
10" x 16" x 1" piece white Styrofoam
Serrated kitchen knife
Waxed paper
Founder's Adhesive glue
Candy circles in variety of colors
Florist's clay
Pebbles
1 (26") length each grosgrain ribbon: red with white polka dots, blue with white polka dots

Note: The candy that is glued to the Styrofoam shapes is **not** to be eaten.

1. Paint the pots and the dowels white. Let the paint dry. Paint alternating red and green curvy stripes on 1 pot, including the rim. Let the paint dry. **Ask the grown-up** to spray the pot with the varnish.

2. Paint blue curvy stripes on the remaining pot, ending the stripes at the rim. Let the paint dry. Trace the small star pattern on page 60 onto the tracing paper. Cut it out. Transfer the star pattern onto the cardboard scrap. **Ask the grown-up** to cut it out using the craft knife.

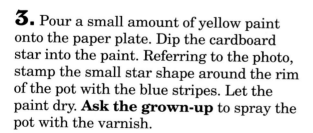

3. Pour a small amount of yellow paint onto the paper plate. Dip the cardboard star into the paint. Referring to the photo, stamp the small star shape around the rim of the pot with the blue stripes. Let the paint dry. **Ask the grown-up** to spray the pot with the varnish.

4. Trace the large star and tree patterns on pages 60 and 61 onto the tracing paper. Using the pencil, transfer the shapes onto the Styrofoam. **Ask the grown-up** to cut out the shapes using the kitchen knife.

5. Using the pencil, poke a 2½"-deep hole in the bottom center of each Styrofoam shape. Insert 1 end of 1 dowel into each hole.

6. Cover the work surface with the waxed paper. Glue candy to 1 side of each Styrofoam shape. Let the glue dry. Turn the shapes over. Glue candy to each remaining side and around the edges. Let the glue dry.

7. Cut 2 (2"-diameter) circles from the cardboard. Place 1 cardboard circle over the hole in the bottom of each pot. Cut 2 (3½"-diameter) circles from the remaining cardboard. Cut an asterisk shape in the center of each circle to slide a dowel through.

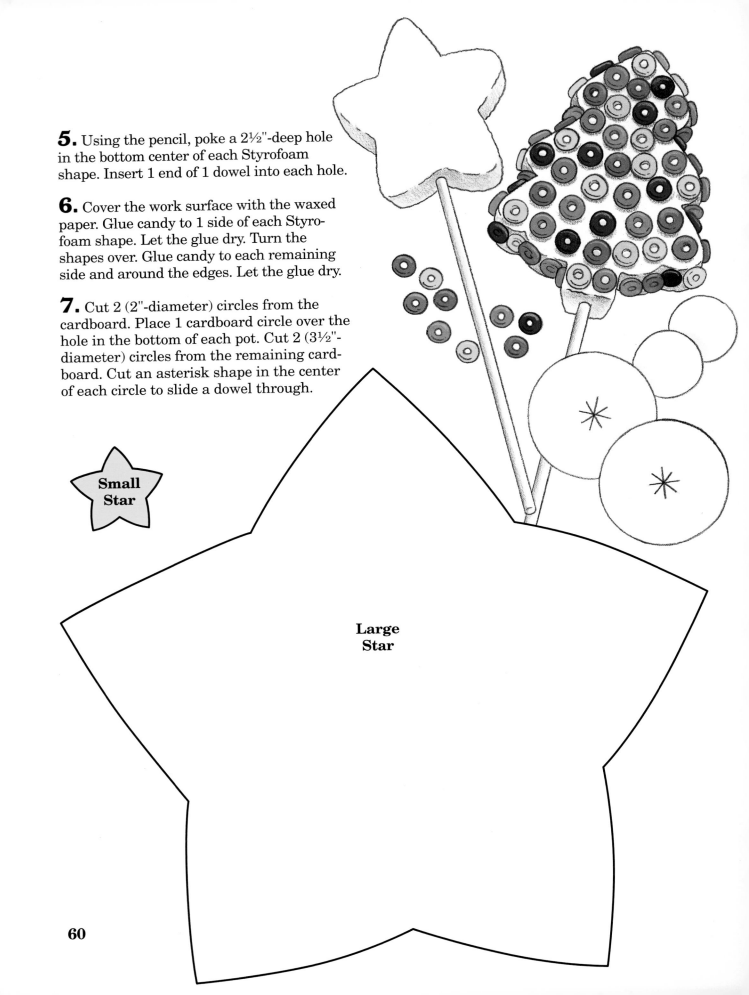

Small Star

Large Star

8. Press a ball of florist's clay on top of the small cardboard circle in each pot. Slide the free end of 1 dowel through each large cardboard circle; then insert the free ends into the balls of florist's clay. Place a handful of pebbles on top of each ball of clay. Slide each large cardboard circle down until it rests securely on top of the pebbles. Fill the remainder of each pot with candy.

9. Tie the red ribbon into a bow around the dowel under the bottom of the tree. Tie the blue ribbon into a bow around the dowel under the bottom of the star.

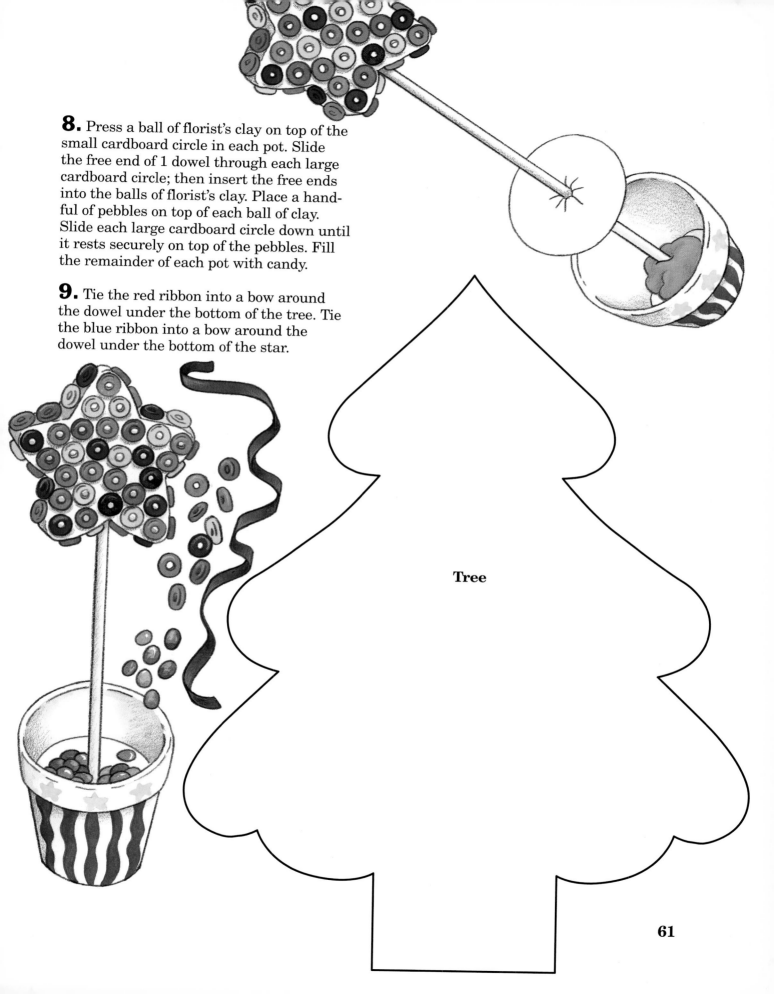

Tree

Candle Accordions

These candle holders are not only pretty and unusual but also very inexpensive. They are easy to make once you get the hang of it, but they can be a little tricky at first, so be sure to practice a few times.

You will need (for each candle holder):
8½" x 11" sheets paper: 1 each of 2
   different colors
Scissors
Craft glue
1½"-diameter candle

Note: Do **not** use construction paper, because it tears too easily. Colored typing paper works well. If the candle does not have a flat bottom, **ask a grown-up** to cut off the point for you so that the candle will stand by itself.

1. Cut 16 (2¾") squares from each piece of paper.

2. Referring to Diagram 1: Fold each square in half. Unfold the squares. Fold each square in half again in the opposite direction. Unfold the squares. Turn the squares over. Fold each square in half diagonally. Unfold the squares.

3. Referring to Diagram 2, pull the diagonal fold corners of 1 square to the center and flatten to make a smaller square. This

smaller square is Unit A. Repeat for all 31 remaining squares.

4. Hold 1 Unit A so that you can look inside it. Put 1 dot of glue on each of the 4 diagonal folds. Referring to Diagrams 3 and 4, tuck 1 Unit A of a different color into the Unit A with glue. The diagonal folds will encase each other. This is Unit B. Repeat with the remaining squares to make 16 Unit Bs. (You may want to practice this step without the glue until you see how the units fit together.)

5. Referring to Diagram 5, join 2 Unit Bs by placing a dot of glue inside 1 outer point of 1 unit and then sliding 1 outer point of another unit over it until the edges are even. Continue until you have 1 Unit B remaining.

6. Shape the joined units into an open circle. Add dots of glue to the 2 remaining outer points. Fit the last Unit B into these points to complete the circle. Let the glue dry.

7. Slip the candle holder over the candle.

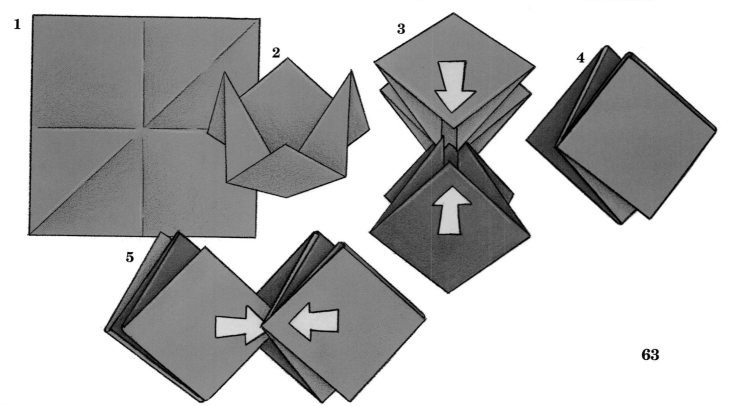

Deck the Doorknobs

All of the elves' doors have decorations much like these hanging from the knobs. They are quick, easy, and as much fun to make as toys!

You will need (for both hangers):
Tracing paper
Pencil
Scissors
Fun Foam: green, red, blue, yellow
¼"-diameter hole punch
Craft glue
For the bell hanger: ½ yard ½"-wide
  striped grosgrain ribbon

1. Trace the patterns on page 66 onto the tracing paper. Cut them out.

2. Transfer the hanger base pattern once to the green foam and once to the red foam. Transfer the bell pattern onto the blue foam, the clapper and star patterns onto the yellow foam, and the tree onto the green

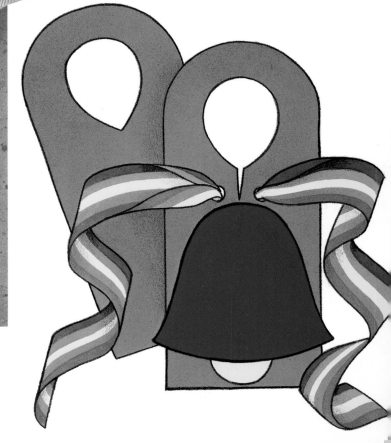

foam. Cut them out. Cut out the circle in the top of each hanger base, being careful not to cut from an outside edge. Using the hole punch, punch 10 dots from the blue foam and 8 dots from yellow foam scraps.

3. **For the bell hanger:** Referring to the photo, center and glue the clapper along the bottom of the green hanger base. Center and glue the bell above the clapper. Cut the slit on the hanger base where indicated on the pattern. Using the hole punch, punch holes in the hanger base where indicated on the pattern. Thread the ribbon through the holes and tie into a bow.

4. **For the tree hanger:** Referring to the photo, center and glue the tree to the red hanger base. Glue the star to the top of the tree. Glue the blue and yellow circles randomly on the tree and the hanger base. Cut the slit on the hanger base where indicated on the pattern.

65

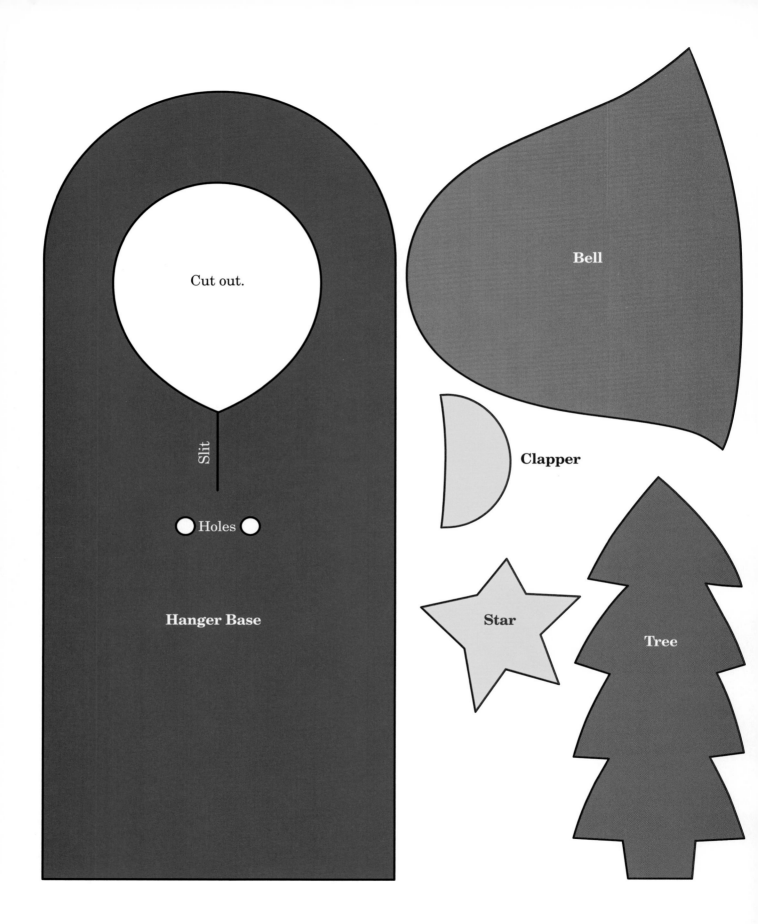

Cut out.

Slit

Holes

Hanger Base

Bell

Clapper

Star

Tree

Golden Twig Candle

Your candle will glow without having to be lit when you embellish it with glittering twigs.

You will need:
Newspaper
Twigs
Gold spray paint
Gold spray glitter
3"-diameter white candle
Founder's Adhesive glue
¾ yard ⅝"-wide gold wire-edged ribbon

1. Cover the work surface with the newspaper. Lay the twigs on the newspaper. Spray 1 side of the twigs with the gold paint. Let the paint dry. Turn the twigs over and spray the other side with the gold paint. Let the paint dry. In the same manner, spray both sides of the twigs with the gold glitter. Let the glitter dry.

2. Break the twigs into lengths equal to the height of the candle.

3. Apply a line of glue around the middle of the candle. Referring to the drawing, press the twigs side by side into the glue around the candle. Make sure the twigs do not extend beyond the base of the candle. Let the glue dry.

4. Wrap the ribbon around the middle of the candle and tie it into a bow. Trim the ribbon ends if necessary.

Level 1

A Cowboy Claus

While Santa usually wears a red cap, sometimes he likes to don a ten-gallon hat. This cowboy card is a unique way to tell your friends, "Ho, Ho, Howdy!"

You will need (for 2 cards):
Tracing paper
Pencil
Carbon paper
8½" x 11" piece card stock
4" x 10" piece sandpaper
Scissors
Fine-tip permanent markers: black, red
Crayons: flesh-colored, pink
Craft glue
4 (7-mm) wiggle eyes
6 (3") lengths red curling ribbon
Iridescent glitter
6 sequin leaves
6 (5-mm) red sequins
2 (5" x 6½") envelopes

1. Trace the Santa, hat crown, and hat brim patterns on page 70 onto the tracing paper. Using the carbon paper, transfer the Santa pattern onto the card stock twice. Place each hat pattern facedown on the smooth side of the sandpaper. Transfer each hat pattern twice. Cut out the shapes. Fold each Santa along the dotted line.

2. Outline the Santas and their features using the black marker. Referring to the photo, fill in the noses and the mouths using the red marker. Using the flesh-colored crayon, color the Santas' faces. Color their cheeks using the pink crayon.

3. Glue the wiggle eyes in place. Referring to the drawing, glue 3 curling ribbon lengths to each Santa for the hatbands. Trim the ribbons to match the Santa shapes. Spread a thin layer of glue on the beard and eyebrow areas. Sprinkle glitter on top of the wet glue. Let the glue dry.

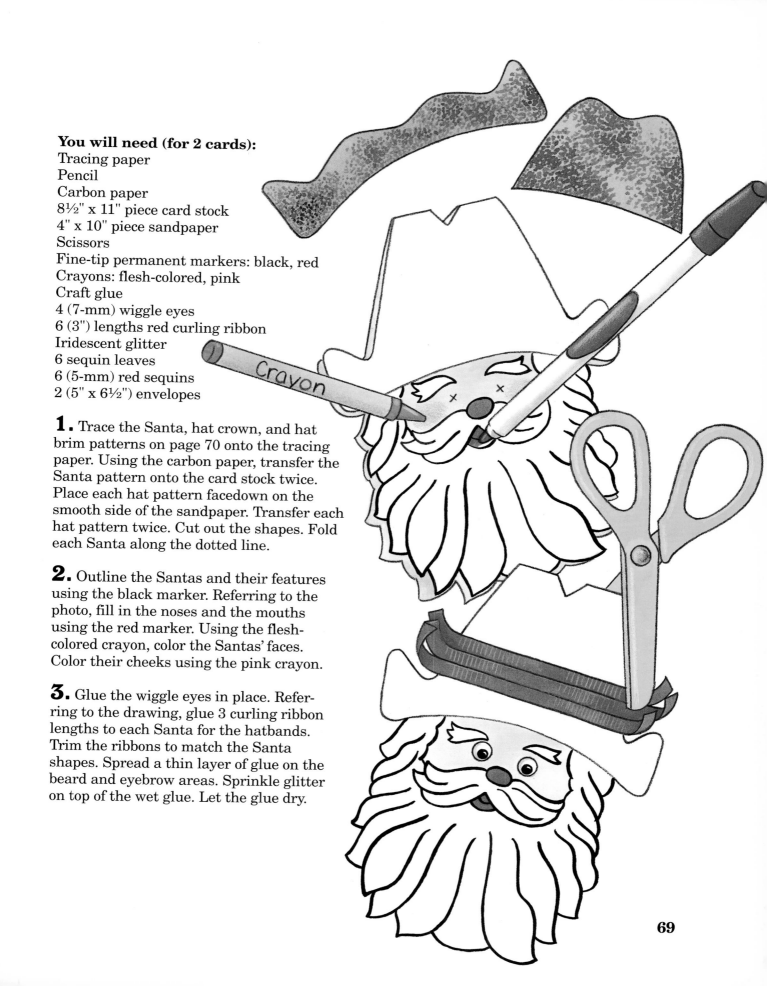

69

4. With the rough side up, glue 1 set of sandpaper hat pieces in place on each Santa. Glue 3 sequin leaves to the right side of each Santa hatband. Glue 3 red sequins on top of the leaves. Let the glue dry.

5. Insert 1 card in each envelope when they are ready to be mailed.

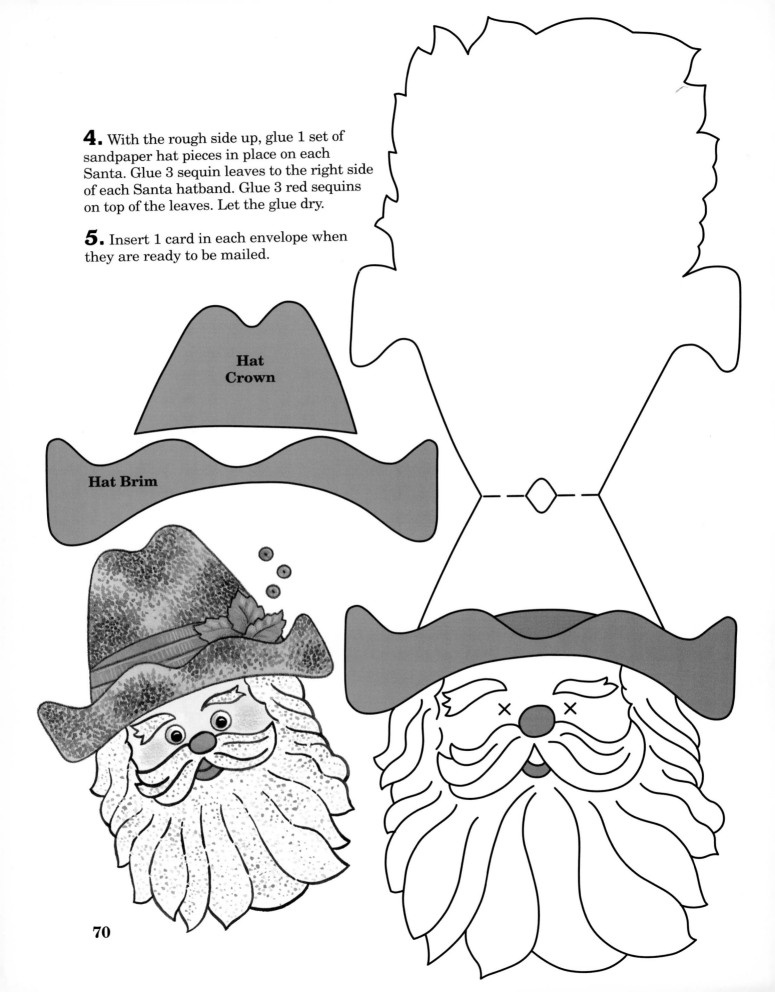

Hat Crown

Hat Brim

Everything That Glitters

These colorful balls will add sparkle and shine to the Christmas tree, and best of all, they won't break like glass balls can!

You will need (for 1 ornament):
Waxed paper
Paper clip
Styrofoam ball of desired size
Glitter paint
Paper plate
Paintbrush
½ yard wire-edged ribbon
Thick craft glue
Scissors

1. Cover the work surface with the waxed paper.

2. For the hanger loop, push the paper clip into the top of the Styrofoam ball until only ¼" of the paper clip remains outside the Styrofoam ball.

3. Squirt a blob of glitter paint onto the paper plate. Use the paintbrush to apply the glitter paint to the Styrofoam ball. Let the paint dry. Apply a second coat of glitter paint if desired; let the paint dry.

4. Tie the ribbon into a bow. Glue the bow in front of the hanger loop. Trim the ribbon ends. Let the glue dry.

Starry Light Switch Plate

This switch plate is an easy way to decorate a room for Christmas. But remember, no turning on the light Christmas Eve night to try to catch a peek at Santa!

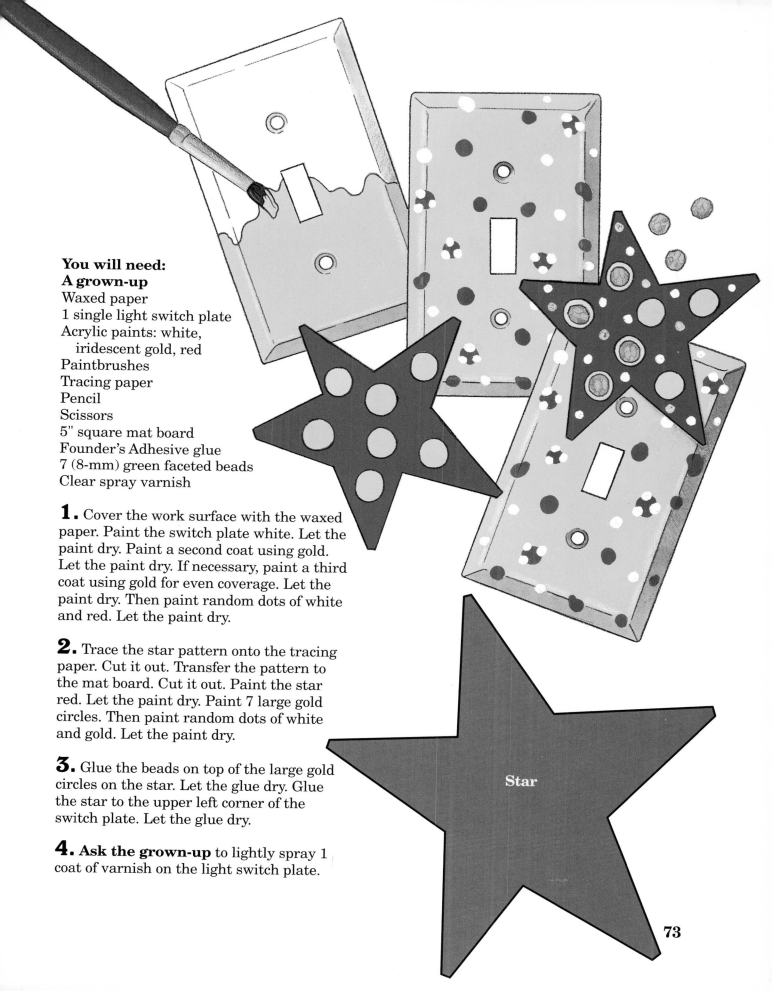

You will need:
A grown-up
Waxed paper
1 single light switch plate
Acrylic paints: white,
  iridescent gold, red
Paintbrushes
Tracing paper
Pencil
Scissors
5" square mat board
Founder's Adhesive glue
7 (8-mm) green faceted beads
Clear spray varnish

1. Cover the work surface with the waxed paper. Paint the switch plate white. Let the paint dry. Paint a second coat using gold. Let the paint dry. If necessary, paint a third coat using gold for even coverage. Let the paint dry. Then paint random dots of white and red. Let the paint dry.

2. Trace the star pattern onto the tracing paper. Cut it out. Transfer the pattern to the mat board. Cut it out. Paint the star red. Let the paint dry. Paint 7 large gold circles. Then paint random dots of white and gold. Let the paint dry.

3. Glue the beads on top of the large gold circles on the star. Let the glue dry. Glue the star to the upper left corner of the switch plate. Let the glue dry.

4. Ask the grown-up to lightly spray 1 coat of varnish on the light switch plate.

Star

Fruit Basket Turnover Apron

This apron is as much fun to make as it is to give—you create it by sponge-painting with an apple, a pear, a lemon, and an orange! And since you only use half of each fruit, you can have a yummy snack with the leftovers.

You will need:
A grown-up
Firm fruits: apple, pear, lemon, orange
Sharp knife
Paper towels
Waxed paper
Dimensional fabric paints: red, golden yellow, kelly green, fluorescent green, orange, fluorescent orange, lemon yellow, purple, leaf green
6 paper plates
Fork
Natural-colored canvas apron
Tracing paper
Pencil
Scissors
Pop-up sponge

1. **Ask the grown-up** to cut the apple, the pear, and the lemon in half lengthwise and to cut the orange in half crosswise.

2. Place 1 piece of each fruit, cut side down, on several layers of paper towels to absorb some of the juice. Cover the work surface with the waxed paper.

3. Squirt a blob of red paint a little smaller than the apple half onto 1 paper plate. Add a little golden yellow along the right side of the red paint. Squirt a blob of kelly green a little smaller than the pear half onto another paper plate. Add a little fluorescent green and golden yellow on top of the kelly green paint.

Squirt a blob of orange paint a little smaller than the orange half onto another paper plate. Add a little fluorescent orange on top. Onto a fourth paper plate, squirt a blob of golden yellow a little smaller than the lemon half. Add a little lemon yellow on top.

4. Place the apron, right side up, on top of the waxed paper. Stab the fork securely into the uncut side of the apple half. Holding the fork, dip the apple, cut side down, into the red paint mixture. Move the apple around to make sure the entire surface is covered. Practice stamping on paper a few times before you begin. Place the apple on the apron, positioning as desired. Press firmly on the apple. Remove the apple. Repeat as desired. Let the paint dry. In the same manner, stamp the pear using the green paint mixture, the orange using the orange paint mixture, and the lemon using the yellow paint mixture.

5. Squirt a little purple paint on a clean paper plate. Dip a finger into the paint and stamp the apron to resemble bunches of grapes.

6. Trace the leaf pattern onto the tracing paper. Cut it out. Transfer the pattern to the sponge. Cut it out. Wet the sponge shape. Squeeze out the excess water. Squirt a bit of leaf green onto the remaining paper plate. Dip the leaf-shaped sponge into the green paint. Gently press the sponge onto a clean area of the paper plate to remove the excess paint. Gently press the sponge onto the apron, positioning the leaves as desired. Let the paint dry.

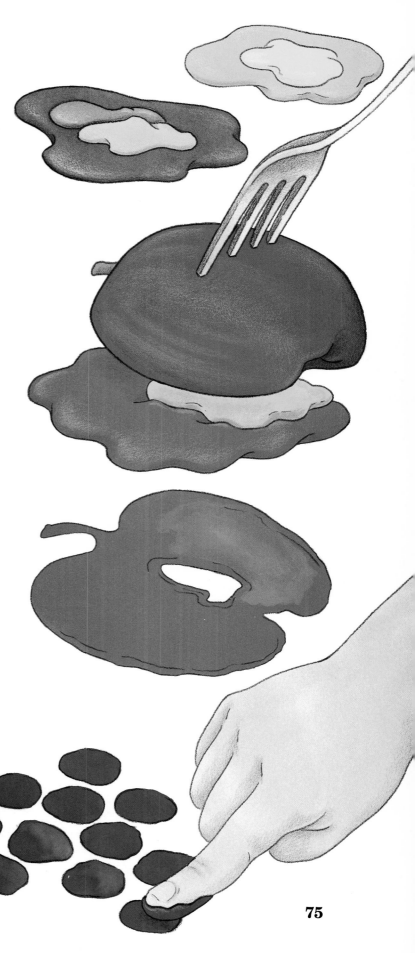

Leaf

Candy Cane Tray

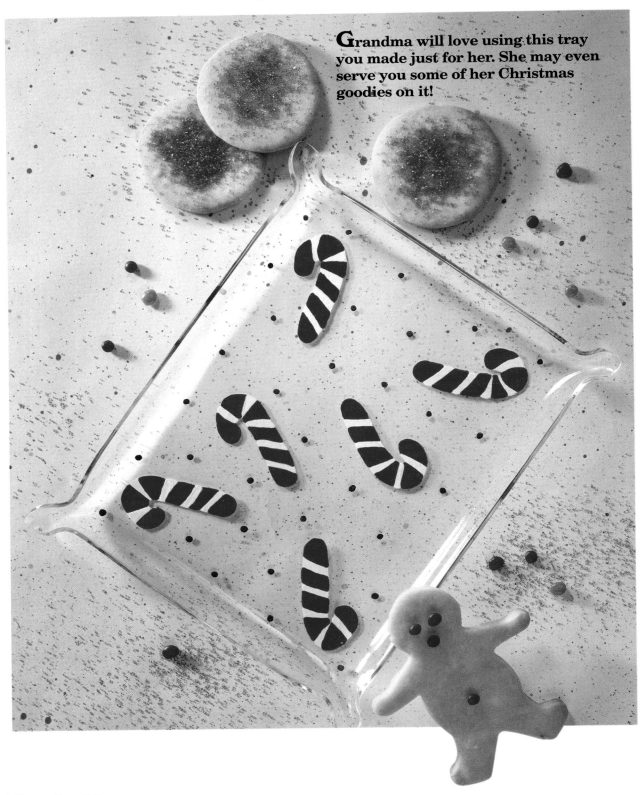

Grandma will love using this tray you made just for her. She may even serve you some of her Christmas goodies on it!

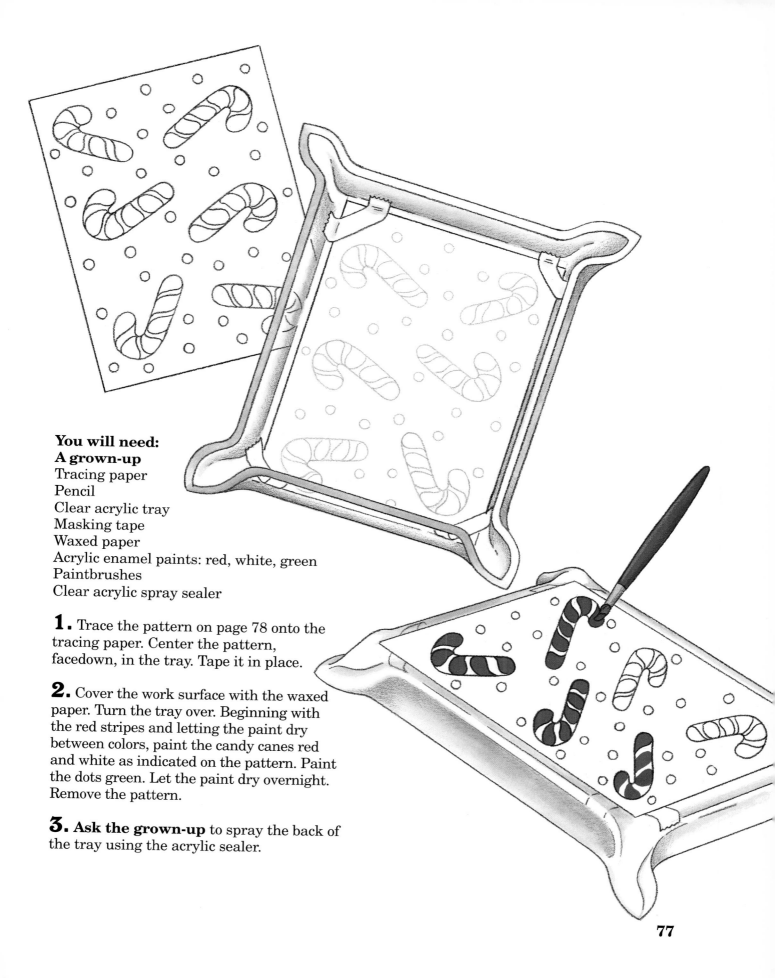

You will need:
A grown-up
Tracing paper
Pencil
Clear acrylic tray
Masking tape
Waxed paper
Acrylic enamel paints: red, white, green
Paintbrushes
Clear acrylic spray sealer

1. Trace the pattern on page 78 onto the tracing paper. Center the pattern, facedown, in the tray. Tape it in place.

2. Cover the work surface with the waxed paper. Turn the tray over. Beginning with the red stripes and letting the paint dry between colors, paint the candy canes red and white as indicated on the pattern. Paint the dots green. Let the paint dry overnight. Remove the pattern.

3. Ask the grown-up to spray the back of the tray using the acrylic sealer.

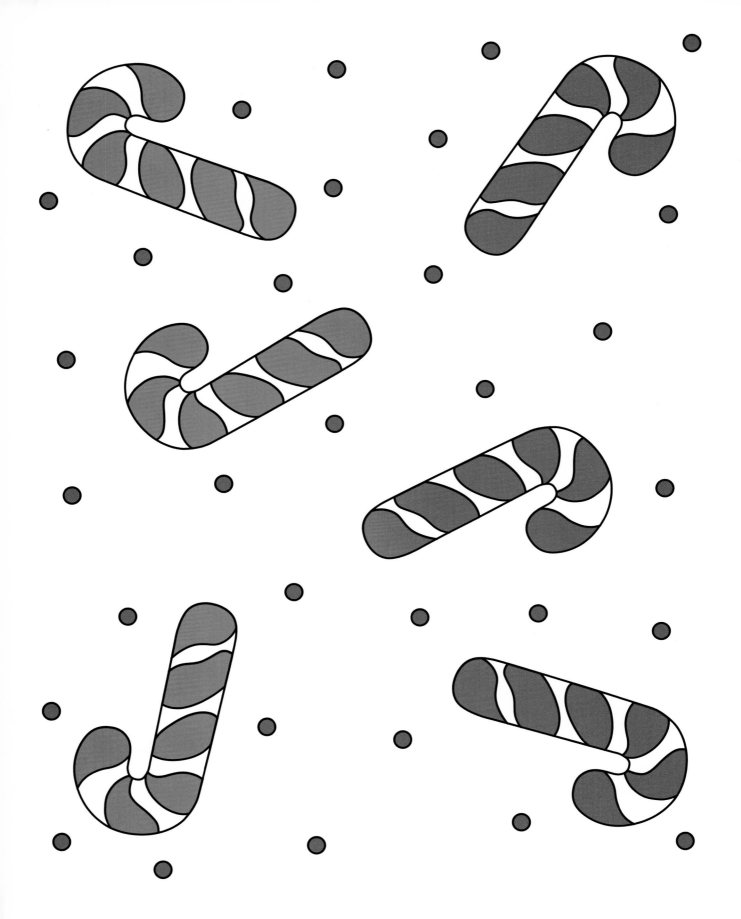

Flowerpot Picture Frame

This whimsical frame has a magnetic personality! By gluing a magnet and washers to the edges, you can create this unique 3-D flowerpot frame.

You will need:
Waxed paper
5" x 7" unfinished wooden picture frame
Acrylic paints: white, iridescent gold,
    magenta, aqua, light purple
Paintbrushes
Black ballpoint pen
Tracing paper
Pencil
Scissors
6" x 12" piece mat board
Founder's Adhesive glue
1 (½"-diameter) heavy-duty round magnet
Flat washers: 1 (1¼"-diameter),
    1 (1¾"-diameter)
6 (8-mm) blue faceted beads

1. Cover the work surface with the waxed paper. Paint the picture frame white. Let the paint dry. Paint a second coat using white. Let it dry. Using a finger, rub gold paint randomly over the white paint on the front of the frame. Before the gold paint dries, use the pen to draw squiggles, circles, and Xs in the paint. Dip 1 fingertip each into the white, magenta, aqua, and light purple paints. Make dots randomly around the front of the frame. Use the gold paint to make dots around the outside edge of the frame. Let the paint dry.

2. Trace the patterns onto the tracing paper. Cut them out. Transfer 1 flowerpot, 3 flowers, and 1 (2") square onto the mat board. Cut them out.

3. Paint the flowerpot in the same manner as the frame. Let the paint dry. Paint 1 flower magenta, 1 aqua, and 1 light purple. Let the paint dry. Paint white dots, squiggles, and lines on the bloom area of each flower. Paint the square white. Let the paint dry. Dip 1 fingertip each into the gold, magenta, aqua, and light purple paints. Make dots and smears on the white square. Let the paint dry.

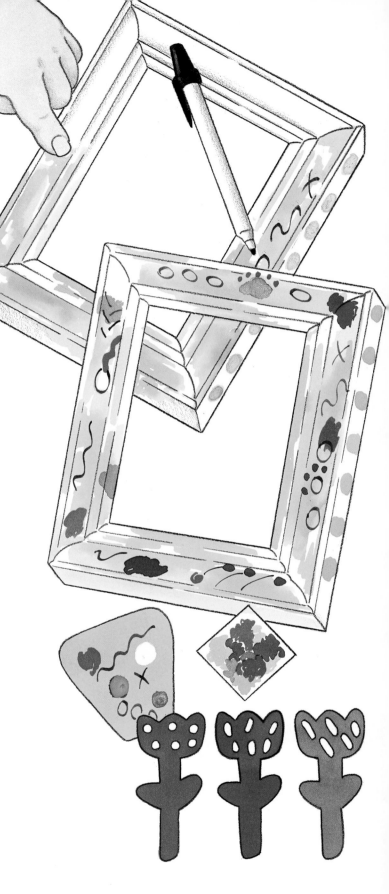

80

4. Glue the 3 flowers stems to the back of the flowerpot as shown. Glue the magnet to the back of the flower stems.

5. Center and glue the 1¼"-diameter washer to the right side of the square. Turn the square so that it is diamond shaped and glue it to the lower right corner of the frame. Glue the beads on top of the washer. Glue the 1¾"-diameter washer to the upper left corner of the frame. Place the magnet-backed flowerpot on the washer.

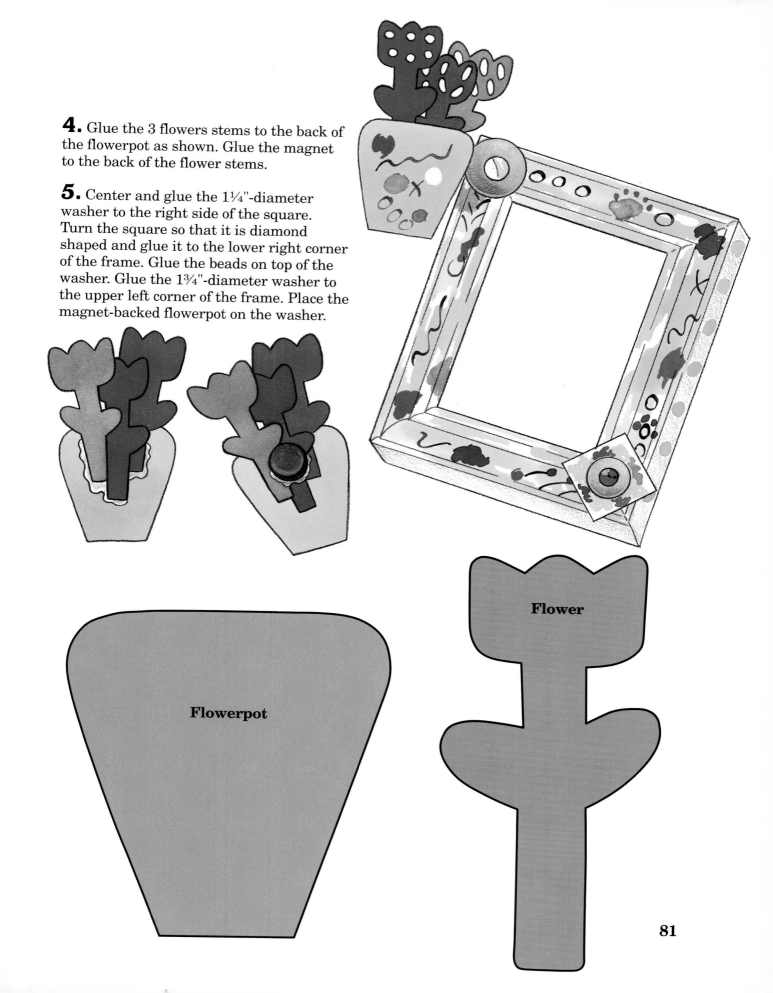

Flowerpot

Flower

81

"Yule-tile" Coasters & Trivet

Sponge-paint plain ceramic tiles and transform them into colorful coasters for the coffee table and a festive trivet to use at the dinner table during the holiday season.

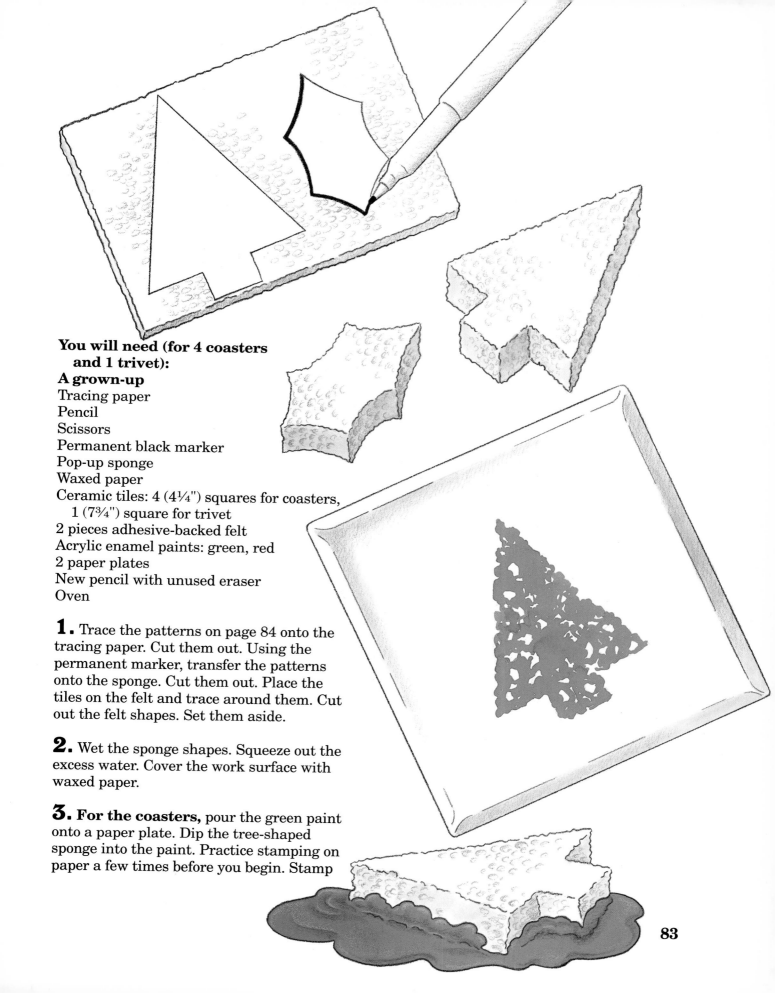

You will need (for 4 coasters and 1 trivet):

A grown-up
Tracing paper
Pencil
Scissors
Permanent black marker
Pop-up sponge
Waxed paper
Ceramic tiles: 4 (4¼") squares for coasters,
    1 (7¾") square for trivet
2 pieces adhesive-backed felt
Acrylic enamel paints: green, red
2 paper plates
New pencil with unused eraser
Oven

1. Trace the patterns on page 84 onto the tracing paper. Cut them out. Using the permanent marker, transfer the patterns onto the sponge. Cut them out. Place the tiles on the felt and trace around them. Cut out the felt shapes. Set them aside.

2. Wet the sponge shapes. Squeeze out the excess water. Cover the work surface with waxed paper.

3. For the coasters, pour the green paint onto a paper plate. Dip the tree-shaped sponge into the paint. Practice stamping on paper a few times before you begin. Stamp

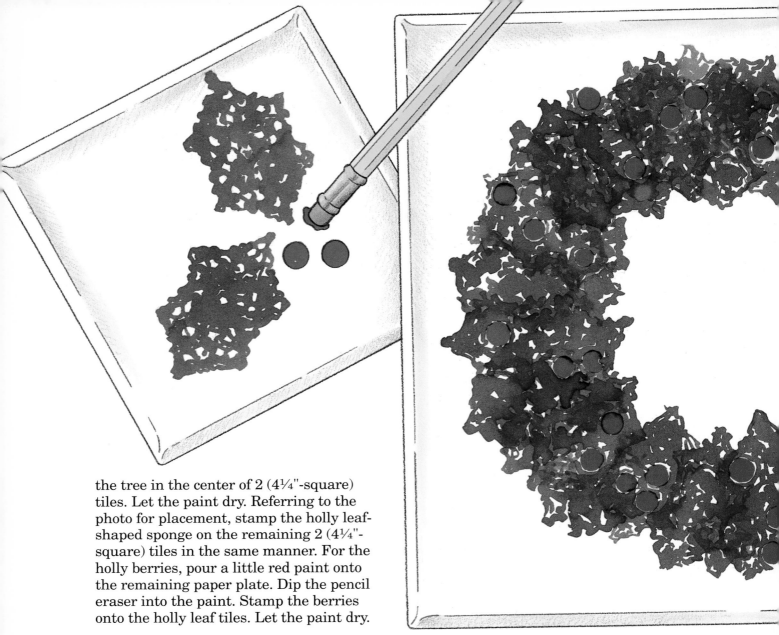

the tree in the center of 2 (4¼"-square) tiles. Let the paint dry. Referring to the photo for placement, stamp the holly leaf-shaped sponge on the remaining 2 (4¼"-square) tiles in the same manner. For the holly berries, pour a little red paint onto the remaining paper plate. Dip the pencil eraser into the paint. Stamp the berries onto the holly leaf tiles. Let the paint dry.

4. **For the trivet,** dip the holly leaf-shaped sponge into the green paint. Stamp the holly leaf onto the 7¾"-square tile to form the shape of a wreath. Let the paint dry. Using the eraser dipped in red paint, add berries to the wreath as desired.

5. **Ask the grown-up** to bake the paint onto the tiles, following the manufacturer's instructions.

6. Let the tiles cool completely. Peel the paper backing off the felt pieces. Stick the felt pieces onto the back of the corresponding tiles.

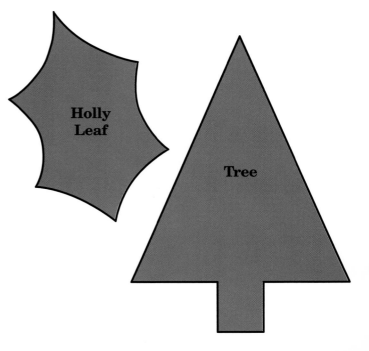

Holly Leaf

Tree

84

Magnetic Mementos

If your mom likes to show off your artwork on the refrigerator, she'll really enjoy displaying it when a picture of you holds it in place! A photograph and a flexible adhesive magnet are all you need to make this personalized decoration.

Level 1

You will need (for 1 magnet):
Scissors
Favorite photograph
Adhesive magnet

1. Cut around the object in the photograph that you want to feature.

2. Peel the backing from the magnet and stick it to the back of the photograph.

3. Trim any excess magnet along the edges of the photograph.

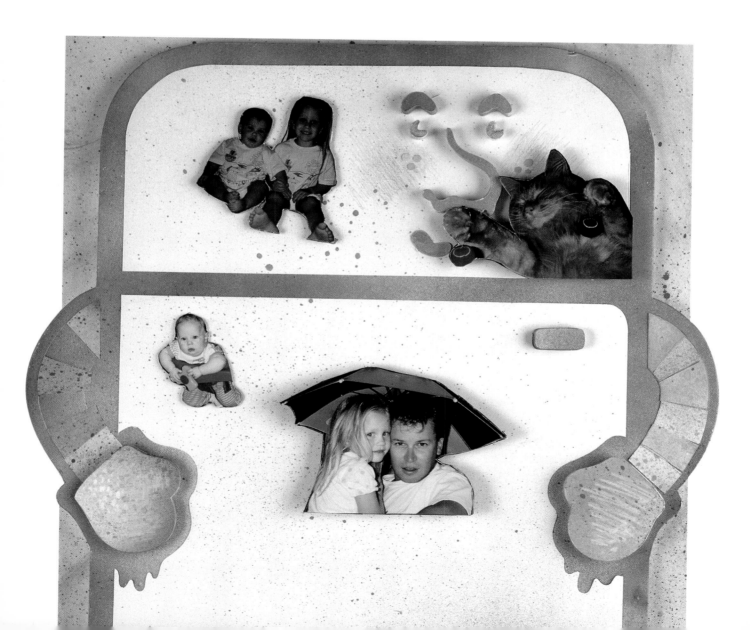

Squeeze & Shape Jewelry

Cutting out Christmas cookies is fun, but cutting out Christmas jewelry is even better—and the treats last a lot longer! Give your friends a present they will love to wear throughout the holidays.

You will need:
A grown-up
Waxed paper
Model Magic™
Zip-top plastic bag
Tiny biscuit cutter or milk jug lid
Scissors
Small cookie cutters or candy molds:
    gingerbread man, star, Christmas tree
Toothpick
Acrylic paints: red, brown, blue, black,
    yellow, green
Small paintbrushes
Founder's Adhesive glue
Iridescent glitter
Spray varnish
Bar pins
Satin cording: 15" to 20" for each necklace

1. Cover the work surface with the waxed paper. Take a small amount of the Model Magic out of the package. Put the remainder in the zip-top bag to keep it fresh. Knead the Model Magic with your fingers until it is soft. Flatten the Model Magic on the waxed paper to approximately ¼" thickness.

2. For the peppermint candy, cut out the shape using the biscuit cutter or the milk jug lid. Trim any rough edges with the scissors. Let both sides of the shape dry.

3. For the gingerbread man, the star, and the Christmas tree, cut out the shapes using the cookie cutters or press the Model Magic into the candy molds. Remove the Model Magic from the cookie cutters or the candy molds. Trim any rough edges. **For the gingerbread man,** make 2 (¼"-diameter) balls, 2 (³⁄₁₆"-diameter) balls, and 1 (⅝"-long) string. Press the ¼"-diameter balls into the gingerbread man body for the buttons. Press the ³⁄₁₆"-diameter balls into

the gingerbread man face for the eyes. Curve the string and press it into the gingerbread man face for the mouth. **For the Christmas tree,** make 4 or 5 (3/16"-diameter) balls. Press the balls into the tree for ornaments. Let both sides of each shape dry.

4. **For the wrapped candy,** make a 3/4"-diameter ball. Flatten 1 side on the waxed paper. Make a 3/4" x 1" rectangle. Cut the rectangle in half to make 2 (1/2" x 3/4") pieces. Pinch 1 end of each piece as shown. Press the pinched ends into opposite sides of the ball as shown. Using the toothpick, make 3 diagonal lines across the pinched pieces to create "folds." Let both sides of the shape dry.

5. **For the peppermint candy,** beginning in the center and painting outward, paint 9 red swirls on the shape. **For the gingerbread man,** paint the body brown; paint the buttons blue; paint the mouth red; and paint black dots in the center of the eyes. **For the star,** paint the shape yellow. **For the Christmas tree,** paint the shape green and paint the ornaments as desired. **For the wrapped candy,** paint the ball area as desired. Let the paint dry. Apply a thin coat of glue to the top of the wrapped candy. Sprinkle glitter onto the glue. Let the glue dry. When completely dry, **ask the grown-up** to spray the shapes with varnish. Let the varnish dry.

6. Glue a bar pin to the back of each shape, even if you are making a necklace. To attach each desired shape to the necklace, open the bar pin completely. Place the cording under the hinge and close the pin. (This will hold each shape in place on the cording.) Space the shapes along the cording as desired.

Marble Barrette

Once you have finished playing marbles, take some of the beautiful glass balls and transform them into a unique hairpiece.

You will need:
⅜" x 3" plain barrette
Founder's Adhesive glue
4 (½"-diameter) marbles

1. Apply a line of glue to the top of the barrette.

2. Press the marbles, 1 at a time, into the glue. Let the glue dry.

Level 1

Merry Mittens

Here comes Santa Claus! And wherever you go, he'll go, too! Everyone will want a pair of these jolly ol' mittens to help keep warm during the holiday season.

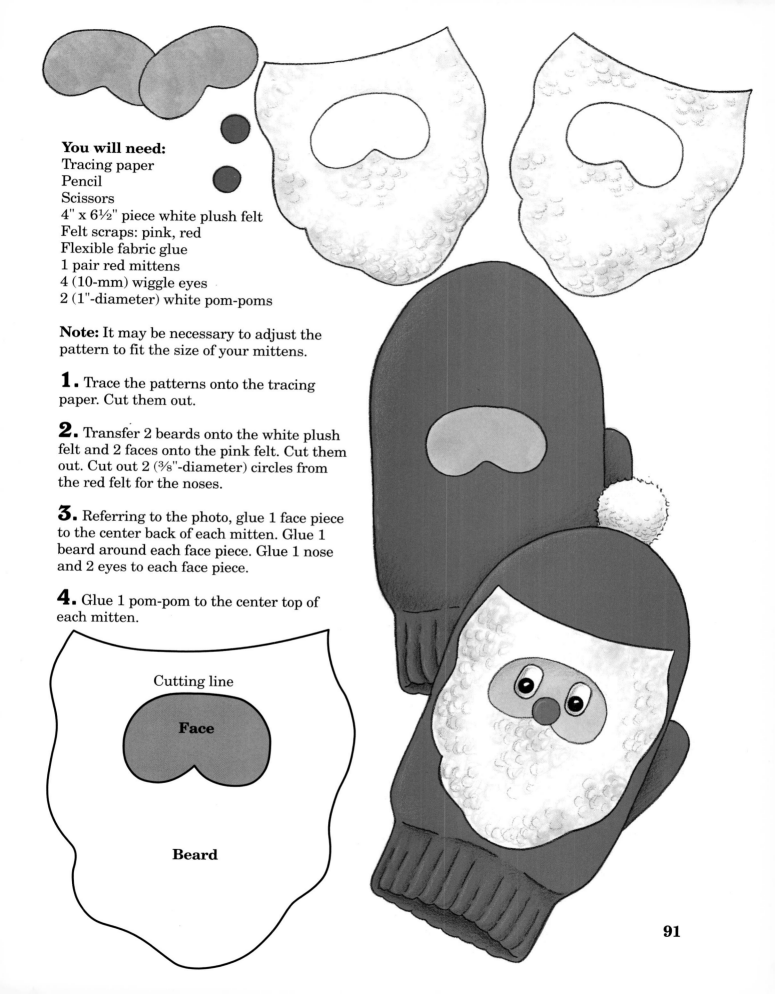

You will need:
Tracing paper
Pencil
Scissors
4" x 6½" piece white plush felt
Felt scraps: pink, red
Flexible fabric glue
1 pair red mittens
4 (10-mm) wiggle eyes
2 (1"-diameter) white pom-poms

Note: It may be necessary to adjust the pattern to fit the size of your mittens.

1. Trace the patterns onto the tracing paper. Cut them out.

2. Transfer 2 beards onto the white plush felt and 2 faces onto the pink felt. Cut them out. Cut out 2 (⅜"-diameter) circles from the red felt for the noses.

3. Referring to the photo, glue 1 face piece to the center back of each mitten. Glue 1 beard around each face piece. Glue 1 nose and 2 eyes to each face piece.

4. Glue 1 pom-pom to the center top of each mitten.

Cutting line

Face

Beard

Glitzy Goggles & Cool Cords

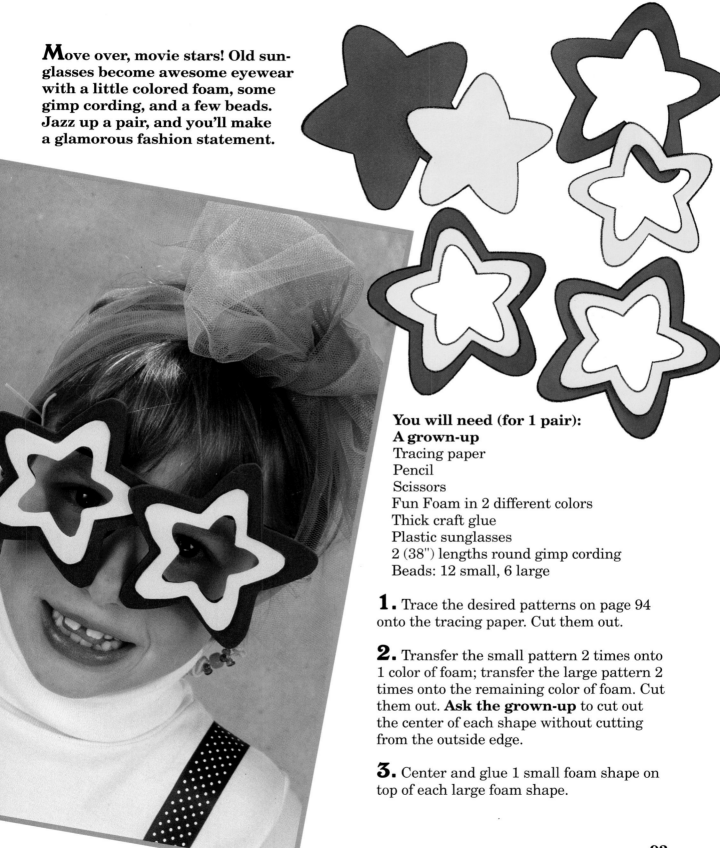

Move over, movie stars! Old sunglasses become awesome eyewear with a little colored foam, some gimp cording, and a few beads. Jazz up a pair, and you'll make a glamorous fashion statement.

You will need (for 1 pair):
A grown-up
Tracing paper
Pencil
Scissors
Fun Foam in 2 different colors
Thick craft glue
Plastic sunglasses
2 (38") lengths round gimp cording
Beads: 12 small, 6 large

1. Trace the desired patterns on page 94 onto the tracing paper. Cut them out.

2. Transfer the small pattern 2 times onto 1 color of foam; transfer the large pattern 2 times onto the remaining color of foam. Cut them out. **Ask the grown-up** to cut out the center of each shape without cutting from the outside edge.

3. Center and glue 1 small foam shape on top of each large foam shape.

93

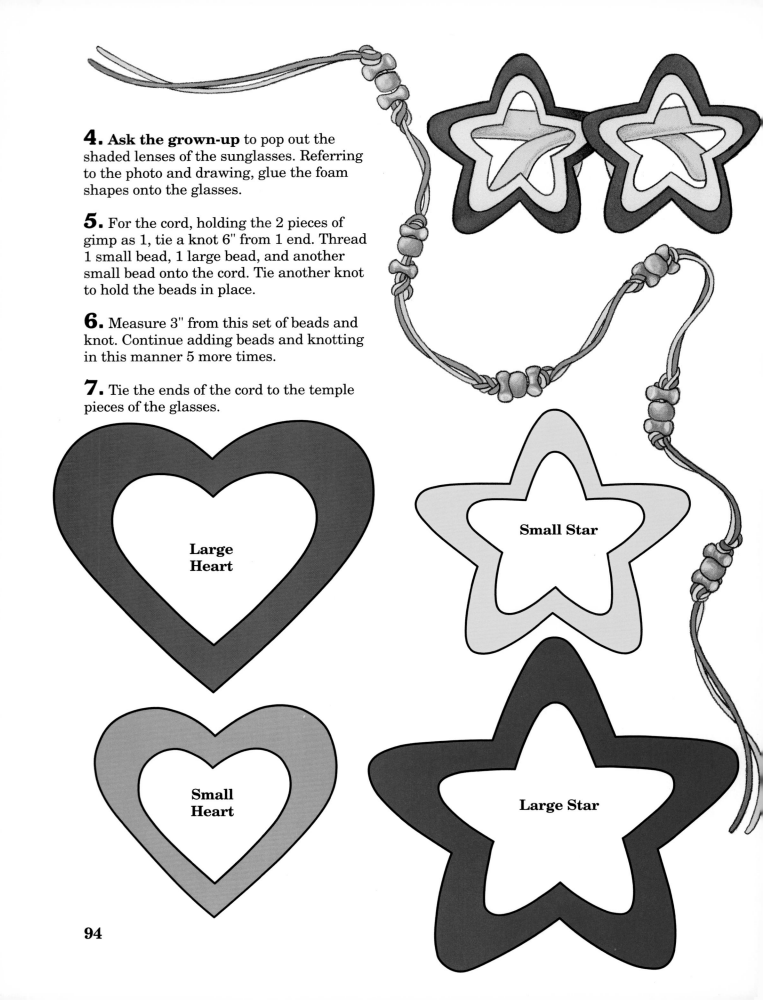

4. Ask the grown-up to pop out the shaded lenses of the sunglasses. Referring to the photo and drawing, glue the foam shapes onto the glasses.

5. For the cord, holding the 2 pieces of gimp as 1, tie a knot 6" from 1 end. Thread 1 small bead, 1 large bead, and another small bead onto the cord. Tie another knot to hold the beads in place.

6. Measure 3" from this set of beads and knot. Continue adding beads and knotting in this manner 5 more times.

7. Tie the ends of the cord to the temple pieces of the glasses.

Large Heart

Small Heart

Small Star

Large Star

94

Space Straws & Moon Rock Shake

Creating these celestial straws is heavenly fun. They are ideal for sipping our out-of-this-world shake. Be sure to include the recipe when you give the straws.

You will need (for 3 straws):
Tracing paper
Pencil
Scissors
Fun Foam: red, orange, purple, blue
Paint pens or glitter glue
Thick craft glue
Metallic curling ribbon
3 drinking straws

1. Trace the patterns onto the tracing paper. Cut them out.

2. Transfer the patterns onto the color foam indicated. Cut them out. Cut slits in the shapes where indicated on the patterns.

3. Decorate the shapes as desired, using the paint pens or the glitter glue. Let the paint or the glue dry.

4. Slide the planet inside the planet ring and glue it in place. Let the glue dry. Pull curling ribbon through the small slits on the lower edge of the rocket and the star. Gently pull the ribbons over a scissors blade to curl. Referring to the photo, insert a drinking straw through the center slits in each shape.

Moon Rock Shake
You will need (for approximately 4 cups):
A grown-up
3 cups softened vanilla ice cream
½ cup whole milk
3 tablespoons honey
Electric blender
Spatula
½ cup almond brickle chips

1. Combine the ice cream, the milk, and the honey in the container of an electric blender.

2. Ask the grown-up to blend the mixture until it is smooth, stopping the blender once to scrape down the sides of the container with the spatula. Add the almond brickle chips to the mixture and blend. Pour the mixture into cups and serve immediately with Space Straws.

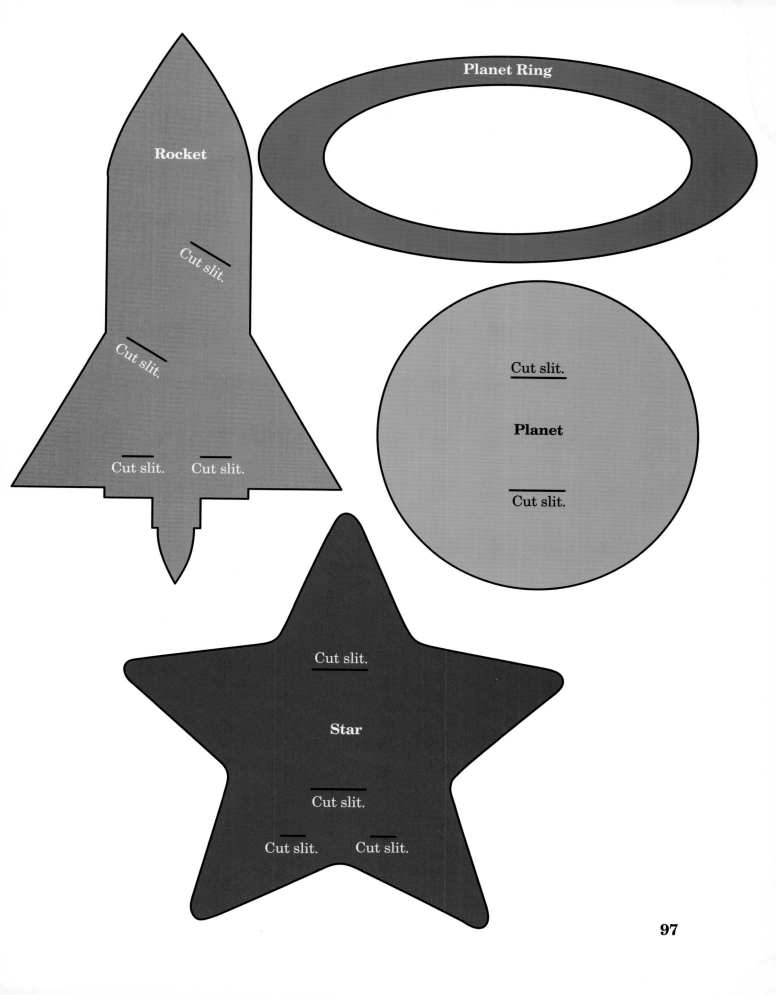

Rocket

Cut slit.

Cut slit.

Cut slit.   Cut slit.

Planet Ring

Cut slit.

Planet

Cut slit.

Cut slit.

Star

Cut slit.

Cut slit.   Cut slit.

Picture-Perfect Greenery

Glue freshly picked greenery inside a papier-mâché covered frame, and you have created a neat, natural wall decoration.

You will need:
A grown-up
Purchased frame with wide border
Waxed paper
Acrylic spray sealer (optional)
White papier-mâché pulp
Heavyweight watercolor paper (cut to
   match frame backing)
Scissors
Pencil
Ruler
Gold paint pen
Thick craft glue
Fresh greenery

1. Remove the backing from the frame and
set it aside. Cover the work surface with
the waxed paper. If the frame is stained or
painted, **ask the grown-up** to spray the
frame with the acrylic sealer to keep the
stain or the paint from bleeding through
the papier-mâché. Let the sealer dry.

2. Following the manufacturer's instructions, mix the papier-mâché. Using your
hands, apply 1 coat of papier-mâché to the
front and the sides of the frame. Let it dry.
Apply a second coat. Let it dry. If necessary,
apply a third coat of papier-mâché for dense
coverage. Let it dry.

3. Place the watercolor paper inside the
frame. Check the fit and trim if necessary.
Using the pencil and the ruler, measure
and lightly mark a line on the watercolor
paper ½" from each inside edge of the
frame. Remove the watercolor paper. Using
the paint pen and the ruler, draw over the
marked lines. Let the paint dry.

4. Assemble the frame. Glue the greenery
onto the watercolor paper as desired.

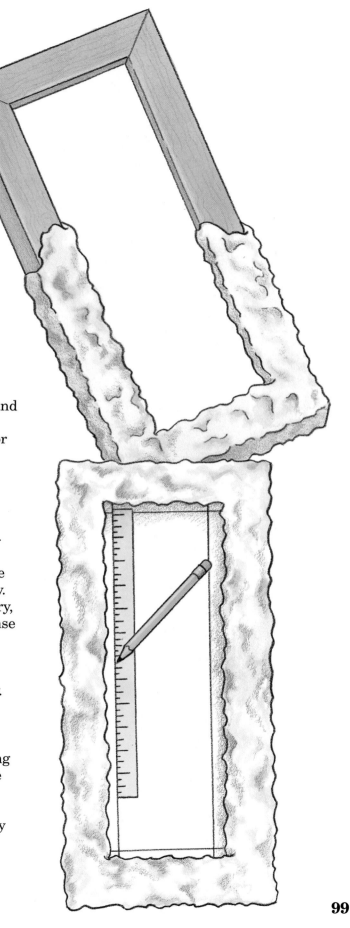

Parents' Workshop
Great Gifts for Children

Cutaway Snowman Vest

A special girl needs a special vest for all of her holiday parties. Make this unique snowman vest by cutting one fabric layer away from another.

You will need:
Purchased vest pattern
Tracing paper
Pencil
Scissors: regular, embroidery
Vanishing fabric marker
Fleece fabric: ⅝ yard to 1 yard blue; 9" x
    10" piece white; 1 (½" x 14") strip each
    red, yellow, and green; 3½" x 5½" scrap
    black; orange and red scraps
⅝ yard to 1 yard blue print fabric for lining
Thread: clear plastic, blue
Sewing machine
Ruler
Liquid ravel preventer
3 medium-sized green sequin leaves
Beads: 3 (6-mm) red, 5 (6-mm) black,
    5 (8-mm) black
Sequin snowflakes
2 packages medium white rickrack

1. Cut out the vest back pattern from the
blue fleece. Using the pencil, trace the
snowman, hat, hatband, and nose patterns
on page 104 onto the tracing paper. Cut
them out along the outside cutting lines.
Using the vanishing fabric marker, transfer
the snowman pattern to the white fleece,
the hat pattern to the black fleece, the
hatband pattern to the red fleece scrap, and
the nose pattern to the orange fleece scrap.
Cut them out.

2. Stack the red, yellow, and green fleece
strips. Using the clear thread, stitch
through all layers ¾" from 1 end. Braid the
strips to within ¾" of the opposite end.
Stitch to secure. Fringe both cut ends.
Stretch the braided section along a ruler to
measure 10". Using the vanishing fabric
marker, mark the braid 6" from 1 end.
Stitch across the braid on each side of the
mark. Cut the braid along the mark.

3. Referring to the photo and the pattern
for placement and using the clear thread:
Handstitch the hatband to the hat. Stitch
the hat to the snowman. Stitch the braided
scarf pieces to the snowman.

4. Center the snowman facedown (with the
scarf toward the center) on the wrong side of
the vest back piece. Using the blue thread,
stitch around the snowman. From the right
side of the vest back piece, use the embroidery scissors to *carefully* cut away the blue
fleece along the inside cutting line to reveal
the snowman. Apply liquid ravel preventer
to the cut edges.

5. Referring to the photo and the pattern
for placement and using the clear thread:
Handstitch the nose in place. Stitch the
leaves and the red beads in place on the hat
brim. Stitch the 6-mm black beads in place
for the mouth. Stitch the 8-mm black beads
in place for the eyes and the buttons. Cross
the braids and tack the scarf.

6. Follow the pattern instructions to
complete cutting and stitching the vest.

7. Tack the sequin snowflakes on the vest
as desired. Stitch the rickrack around the
edges of the vest.

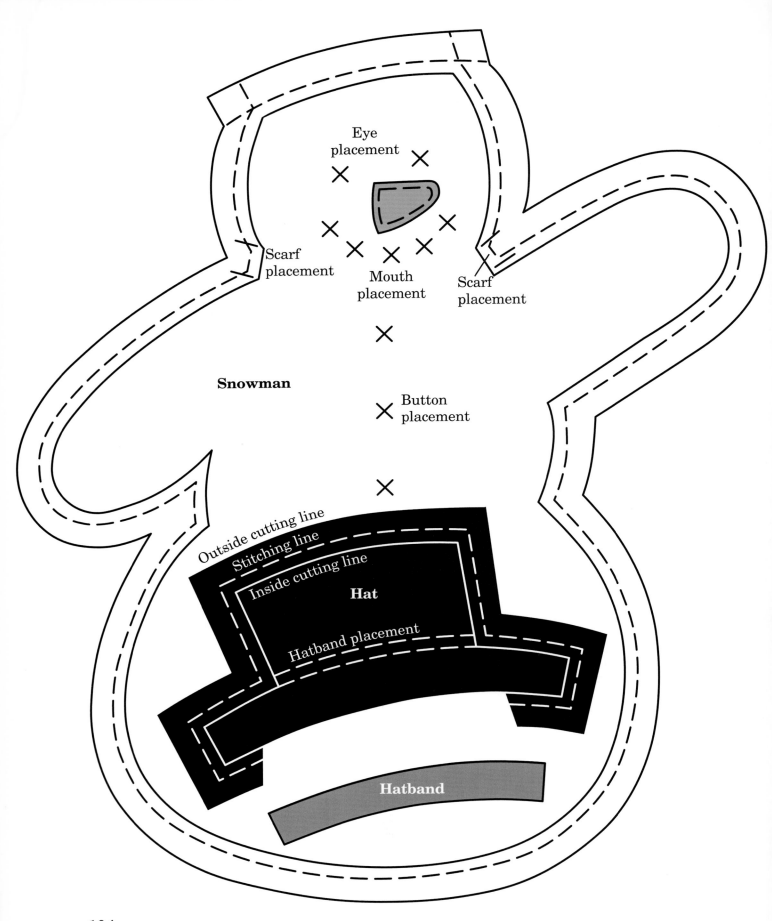

Eye placement

Scarf placement

Mouth placement

Scarf placement

Snowman

Button placement

Outside cutting line

Stitching line

Inside cutting line

Hat

Hatband placement

Hatband

Santa Snuggler

This corduroy Santa blanket is perfect for wrapping up your jolly little elf while reading "A Visit from St. Nicholas."

You will need:

Red pinwale corduroy: 1 (15") square, 2 (45") squares
Scissors
White thread
5¾ yards 1"-wide white double-fold bias tape
Sewing machine
Straight pins
1 (3"-diameter) white pom-pom

1. Fold the 15" square in half diagonally, aligning the sides. Cut along the diagonal fold. With the wrong sides facing and the raw edges aligned, stack the triangular pieces.

2. Bind the longest edge of the triangle with the bias tape.

3. With the wrong sides facing and the raw edges aligned, stack the 45" squares on a flat surface and pin them together. Referring to the photo, for the hood, position the triangular piece in 1 corner, aligning the raw edges. Pin it in place.

4. Bind the raw edges with the remaining bias tape, mitering the corners.

5. Handstitch the pom-pom to the point of the hood.

Flower Children

Your little girl's face will beam when you give her this sunflower collar and whimsical matching doll.

You will need (for the collar):
Tracing paper
Pencil
Scissors
Straight pins
⅓ yard cotton muslin
Sewing machine
¼ yard each cotton fabric: yellow, gold miniprint, green-and-black plaid
Thread to match fabrics
12" length ¼"-wide cream grosgrain ribbon

1. To make the collar pattern, draw a 12"-diameter circle onto the tracing paper, using the pencil. In the center of the circle, draw a 4"-diameter circle. Cut out the large circle and the center circle. (**Do not** cut into the center circle from the outside edge.) With the right sides facing, fold the muslin in half, with the short edges together. Pin the collar pattern to the muslin. Trace around the large circle and the center circle. Cut out the large circle. Pin the muslin layers together.

2. Stitch along the center circle outline, backstitching at the beginning and the end. Fold the large circle in half. To create the back opening, cut through the fold from 1 outside edge through the stitching and into the center circle. Cut out the center circle, leaving a ¼" seam allowance. Clip the curved seam allowance. Turn right side out and press the seam. Staystitch ¼" from the outside edge of each large circle. Press each cut edge of the back opening under ¼".

3. To make the petals, cut 12 (4") squares each from the yellow fabric and the gold miniprint fabric. With the wrong sides facing and the raw edges aligned, fold each square in half diagonally to form a triangle. Press. Fold each point along the fold up to align with the remaining point as shown. Press. With the right sides facing, pin the yellow petals along the outside edge of the top large circle as shown. Then pin the gold miniprint petals on top of and between the yellow petals. Baste.

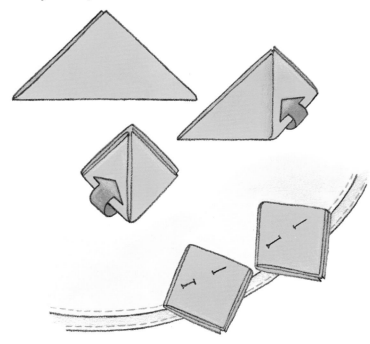

4. Trace the pattern for the collar leaves on page 110 onto the tracing paper, repeating the pattern until it measures 30" long. Transfer the 30"-long leaf pattern to the green-and-black plaid fabric 4 times. With the right sides facing and the raw edges aligned, pin 2 leaf pieces together. Stitch together around the points. Trim the points and clip the seam. Turn the leaves right side out and press. Repeat with the remaining leaf pieces. Slipstitch the lengths together at 1 end. Run gathering stitches

along the long straight edge. With the raw edges aligned, pin the leaves on top of the petals, adjusting the gathers to fit. Baste ¼" from the edge of the circle.

5. Machine-stitch the leaves and the petals in place, leaving the remaining circle piece free. Trim the edges even. Fold the leaves and the petals to the outside and press.

6. Fold the outside edge of the remaining circle piece along the staystitching line. Slipstitch this facing layer to the petal layer along the outside edge.

7. Cut the ribbon length in half. Insert ¼" of 1 end of 1 ribbon length into each inside edge of the back opening. Slipstitch in place. Slipstitch the edges of the back opening closed.

You will need (for the doll):
Tracing paper
Pencil
¾ yard sunflower print cotton fabric
Cotton fabric scraps: yellow, brown
¼ yard green-and-black plaid cotton fabric
Scissors
Straight pins
Sewing machine
Embroidery floss: black, white
Powdered blush
Vanishing fabric marker
Stuffing
Safety pin
12" length ¼"-wide elastic

1. Using the pencil, trace the patterns on pages 110 and 111 onto the tracing paper. Cut them out. Transfer the patterns onto the fabrics as indicated. Cut them out. Cut out 4 (4"-diameter) circles from the brown fabric. From the sunflower fabric, cut a 12" x 45" piece for the skirt and 2 (6½" x 8") pieces for the arms.

2. To make the arms, with the right sides facing and the raw edges aligned, fold 1 arm piece in half lengthwise. Stitch together along the long edge. Turn. Run gathering stitches along 1 short end. Pull tightly to gather. Fold under ¼" of the remaining short end. Baste, leaving a thread tail for gathering. Baste ¼" from the edge of 1 brown circle. Place a small amount of stuffing in the center of the circle on the wrong side. Pull the thread to gather; tie off the thread to secure. Slip the gathered end of the circle inside the open end of the arm. Pull the basting thread in the arm to gather. Tie off the thread to secure. Repeat for the other arm.

3. To make the body, with the raw edges aligned, pin the arms to the right side of 1 doll body piece where indicated. Baste. With right sides facing, the raw edges aligned, and arms toward center, pin the body pieces together. Stitch, catching the arms in the stitching and leaving the straight bottom edge open. Clip the curves. Turn and press. Stuff the body.

4. To make the legs, with the right sides facing and the raw edges aligned, pin 2 leg pieces together. Stitch ¼" from the edge, leaving the top of the leg open. Clip the curves. Turn and press. Fill the bottom 6" of the leg with stuffing. Tie the leg in a knot to form the knee. Then continue stuffing the leg. Repeat for the other leg. Turn ¼" of the bottom edge of the body to the inside. Insert the legs into the body. Slipstitch the opening closed.

5. To make the doll petals and the leaves, with the right sides facing and the raw edges aligned, pin two leaf pieces together. Stitch together around the points. Clip. Turn and press. Repeat for the petals. Run gathering stitches along the long straight edge of the leaf and petal pieces. Pull the threads to gather. Adjust the gathers to form a 2"-diameter circle for each. Referring to the photo and aligning the raw edges, place the petals on top of the leaves; baste. Baste in place on the head area of the body.

6. To stitch the face, using fabric marker, center and transfer the face details to the right side of 1 brown circle. Using 2 strands of black embroidery floss, stemstitch the hair, the eyebrows, the nose, the mouth, and the chin. Satin-stitch the eyes. Using 2 strands of white embroidery floss, straight-stitch the eye accents. Use the blush to add the cheeks. With the right sides facing and the raw edges aligned, pin the remaining brown circle to the face. Stitch ¼" from the edge. Clip the curves. Carefully cut a small slit through the back layer only. Turn the face through the slit. Press. Center and slipstitch the face over the raw edges of the circle of petals and leaves.

7. To make the skirt, with the right sides facing and the raw edges aligned, fold the 12" x 45" sunflower fabric piece in half, with the short edges together. Stitch along the short edge, ¼" from the edge. To make the casing, fold 1 long raw edge under ½" twice. Stitch close to the top and bottom fold. Clip a few stitches of the casing seam on the wrong side of the skirt. Using a safety pin, pull the elastic through the casing. Overlap the ends of the elastic ¾"; whipstitch them together. Try the skirt on the doll to make sure that the skirt fits snuggly. Adjust the elastic if necessary. Work the elastic back inside the casing. Slipstitch the opening closed. Fold the skirt bottom under ½" twice and hem.

Face detail placement

Collar Leaves
Repeat pattern
until 30" long.

Doll Petals/Leaves
Repeat pattern 3 times.
Seam allowance is
included.

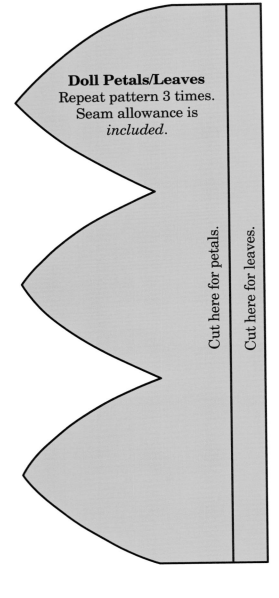

Cut here for petals.

Cut here for leaves.

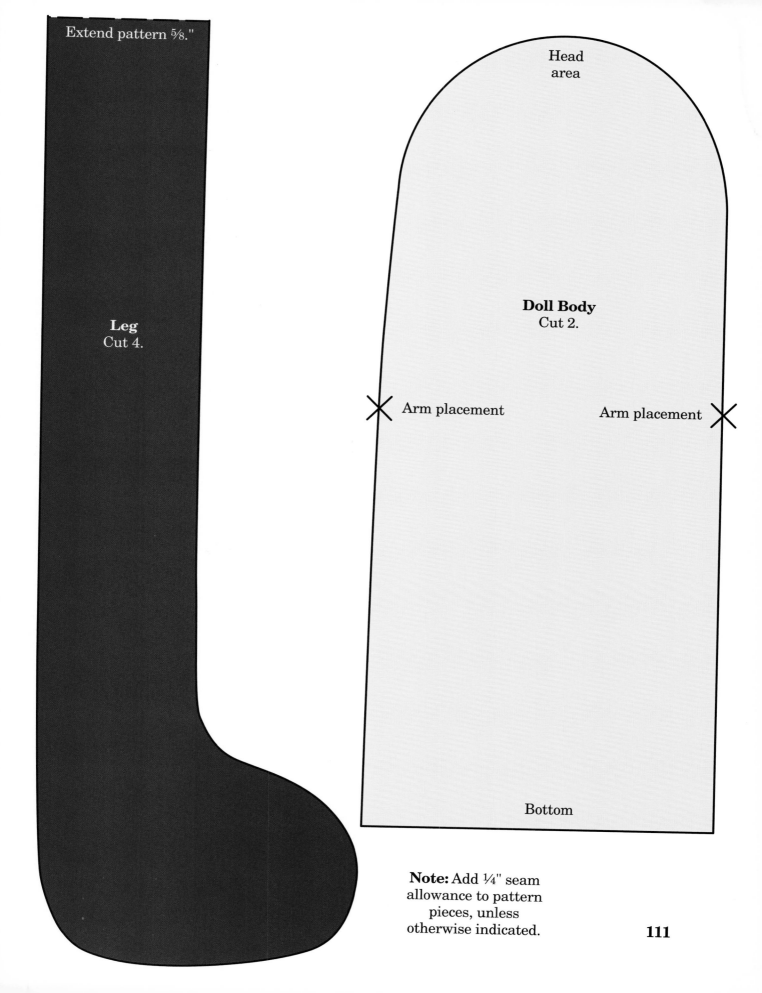

Extend pattern ⅝."

Leg
Cut 4.

Head
area

Doll Body
Cut 2.

Arm placement ✕   ✕ Arm placement

Bottom

Note: Add ¼" seam
allowance to pattern
pieces, unless
otherwise indicated.

111

Sports-Minded Caps

If sports fill his thoughts, he'll want one of these caps upon his head!

You will need (for each cap):
Scissors
Vanishing fabric marker
Iron and ironing board
For the baseball cap: tracing paper, pencil, purchased white cap, 1 package red iron-on patches
For the soccer cap: tracing paper, pencil, purchased black cap, 2 packages white iron-on patches, straight pins
For the basketball cap: purchased orange cap, 2 packages brown iron-on patches

1. **For the baseball cap:** Using the pencil, trace the indicated pattern onto the tracing paper. Cut it out. Using the vanishing fabric marker, transfer the pattern to the red patches approximately 50 to 60 times. Set the iron on a dry setting. Referring to the photo or a baseball for placement, position the patch shapes on the cap. Placing the cap around the small end of the ironing board and following the manufacturer's directions, iron the patch shapes in place.

3. **For the basketball cap:** Cut ⅜"-wide bias strips from the brown patches. Referring to the photo or a basketball for positioning and using the vanishing fabric marker, draw 3 lines from the front of the cap to the back of the cap and 1 line from side to side across the center of the cap. Position the bias patch strips over the guidelines, cutting to fit. Placing the cap around the small end of the ironing board and following the manufacturer's directions, iron the patch strips in place. If the cap has a button on top, cut a small circle from the brown patch scraps and iron it over the button.

Soccer Cap
(Black shape)

2. **For the soccer cap:** Using the pencil, trace the black shape and white shape patterns onto the tracing paper. Cut them out. Using the vanishing fabric marker, transfer the white shape pattern to the white patches approximately 14 times. Referring to the photo, pin the white patch shapes in place, using the black shape pattern to help with spacing. Placing the cap around the small end of the ironing board and following the manufacturer's directions, iron the patch shapes in place.

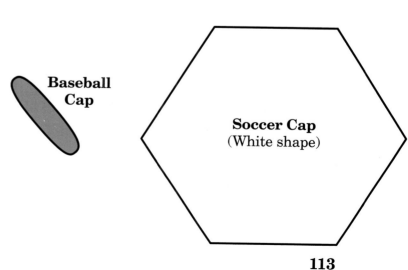

Baseball Cap

Soccer Cap
(White shape)

Sponge-Painted Sweat Jacket

This pretty jacket is just right for those cool days of spring.

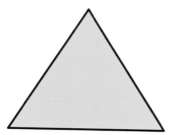

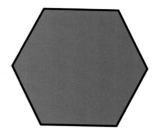

You will need:
Purchased sweatshirt (1 size larger than
   child normally wears)
Ruler
Vanishing fabric marker
Scissors
Thread to match sweatshirt
Hem facing to match sweatshirt
   (approximately 2" wide)
Sewing machine with buttonhole attachment
4 (1⅛") buttons to cover
Tracing paper
Pencil
Pop-up sponges
Waxed paper
Fabric paints in a variety of colors
Paper plates

1. Wash and dry the sweatshirt. Using the
ruler and the vanishing fabric marker,
mark the center front of the sweatshirt.
Cut along this mark to make the front
opening. Cut off the neckband, the sleeve
bands, and the waistband. Staystitch
around the neck and along the front
opening, ¼" from the raw edges. Staystitch
around the bottom, 2½" from the cut edge.

2. To face both sides of the front opening
and the neck, unfold the hem facing; fold the
cut end under ½". With the right sides
facing, the edges aligned, and beginning at
the staystitching line on 1 side of the front
opening, pin the hem facing in a continuous
piece, mitering the corners. Trim the hem
facing at the end 2" from the bottom edge;
fold the cut end under ½". Stitch the hem
facing to the sweatshirt, ¼" from the edge.
Fold the hem facing to the wrong side of the
sweatshirt; pin. Topstitch the facing ¼" from
each edge and again 1½" from each edge.

3. Make 4 buttonholes, centered vertically
along the facing.

4. Try the jacket on the child. Turn the
sleeves under to fit. Topstitch each sleeve
¼" from the lower edge of the hem and
again near the top of the hem.

5. Using the pencil, transfer the shape
patterns onto the tracing paper. Cut them
out. Transfer the patterns to the sponges
and cut them out. Wet the sponge shapes
and squeeze out the excess water.

6. Lay the sweatshirt flat. Using the
vanishing fabric marker, trace the shapes
as desired along the front opening, the
neck, and the sleeves. Place waxed paper
under the front opening and the neck and
inside the sleeves.

7. Pour each color of paint onto a separate
paper plate. Dip each sponge into 1 color of
paint; wipe the excess paint off on the side
of the plate. Sponge-paint the shapes along
the front opening and along the neck. Let
the paint dry. Sponge-paint the front of the
sleeves. Let the paint dry. Then sponge-
paint the shapes on the back of the sleeves.
Let the paint dry.

8. Following the manufacturer's instructions, cover the buttons with sweatshirt
scraps. Stitch the buttons in place along the
left side of the front opening.

9. Fringe the bottom edge of the sweatshirt
by cutting 2¼"-long slits every ½". Be careful
not to cut through the staystitching line.

Christmas Bibs

Your little one will be a "star" during the "holly-days" when he wears one of these festive bibs.

You will need (for each bib):
Tracing paper
Pencil
Scissors
Vanishing fabric marker
Sewing machine
For the holly leaf bib: 10" x 14" piece
each green cotton fabric, green-and-white
print cotton fabric for lining, and ⅛"-
thick batting; red cotton fabric scrap;
paper-backed fusible web scrap; red and
green thread; 1 yard ½"-wide green bias
tape
For the star bib: 14½" x 15½" piece each
yellow cotton fabric, yellow-and-white
print cotton fabric for lining, and ⅛"-
thick batting; white and yellow thread;
zipper foot; 1¼ yard white corded piping;
1 yard ½"-wide white bias tape

1. Using the pencil, trace the desired pattern on pages 118 and 119 onto the tracing
paper. Cut it out. Using the vanishing fabric
marker, transfer the pattern to the solid-
colored fabric, the lining fabric, and the
batting, adding a ½" seam allowance around
the outside edge. Cut the pieces out. Cut
along the back closure line and cut out the
center circular neckline.

2. For the holly leaf bib: Using the
tracing paper and the pencil, trace 1 holly
berry pattern. Cut it out. Following the
manufacturer's instructions, fuse the
fusible web scrap to the wrong side of
the red fabric scrap. Using the vanishing
fabric marker, transfer the berry pattern
to the fused fabric scrap 3 times. Cut them
out. Referring to the pattern and the photo,
fuse the berries in place on the right side of
the solid green piece. Using the red thread,
machine-appliqué around the berries, using
a zigzag stitch.

3. For the star bib: With the edges
aligned, use the zipper foot and the yellow
thread to stitch the piping to the right side
of the solid yellow star piece along the
outside edge.

4. With the right sides facing and the raw
edges aligned, stack the solid fabric piece,
the lining piece, and the batting. Using
matching thread, stitch through all the
layers, leaving an opening for turning. Trim
the seams and clip the curves. Turn.

5. Placing the center of the bias tape at
the center mark on the bib, encase the raw
neck edges with the bias tape. (The bias
tape will extend beyond the bib to create
the neck ties.) Unfold each cut end of the
bias tape and fold it under ¼". Refold.
Beginning and ending at 1 free end and
using matching thread, stitch along the
open edges, encasing the neckline.

6. Machine-quilt the bib as indicated on
the pattern.

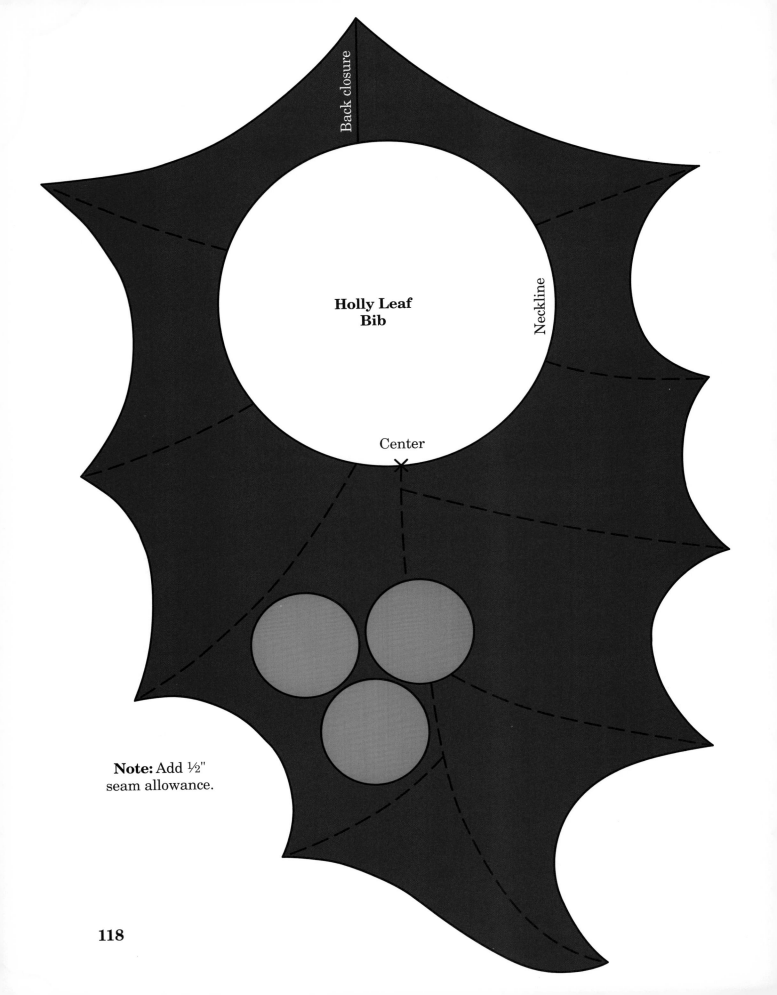

Back closure

Holly Leaf
Bib

Neckline

Center

Note: Add ½"
seam allowance.

118

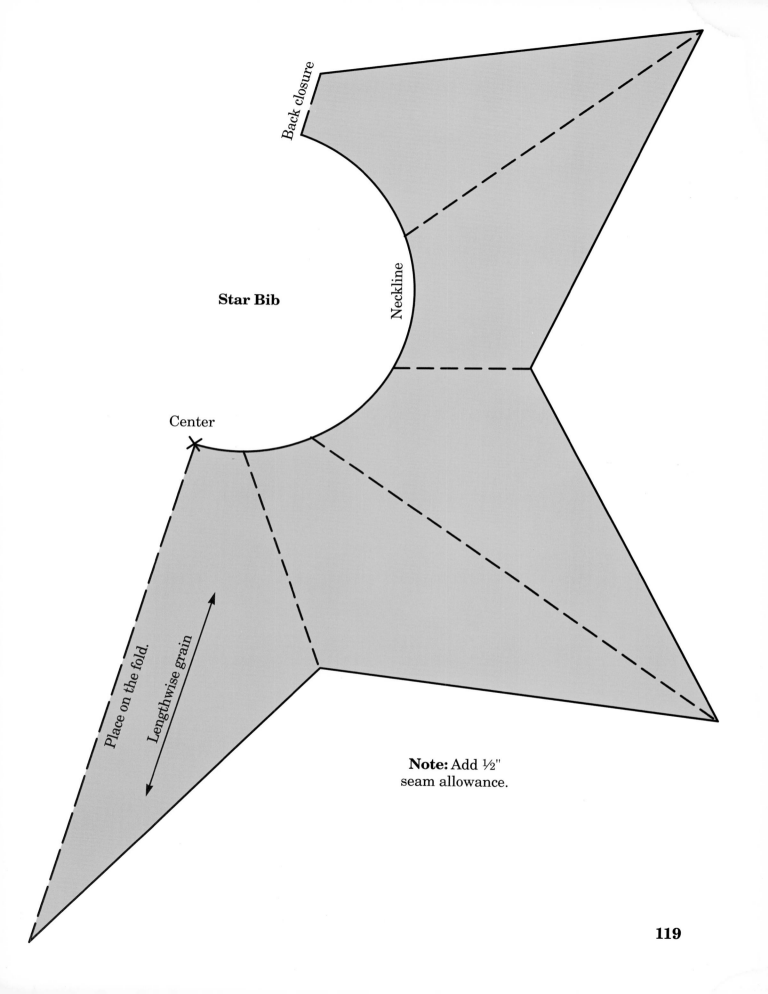

Star Bib

Back closure

Neckline

Center

Place on the fold.

Lengthwise grain

Note: Add ½"
seam allowance.

Tree-Trimming Shoes

Set her feet to dancing with these holiday sneakers! Best of all, these shoes are so easy to create—they're made using stickers!

You will need:
Red canvas tennis shoes
Assorted Christmas stickers
Waxed paper
Washable glue
1" sponge brush
2 (1-yard) lengths each ⅛"-wide ribbon: red,
    green, white
Scissors
Masking tape

Note: Wash and dry the tennis shoes before embellishing them.

1. Remove the shoelaces from the shoes and reserve them for another use. Arrange the stickers on the shoes as desired.

2. Cover a table with the waxed paper to protect the surface. Lift a sticker off 1 shoe and use your finger to spread a thin layer of glue on the shoe under the sticker. Smooth the sticker over the glue and then spread a thin layer of glue over the sticker. Repeat for each sticker. Cover the entire shoe with glue, being careful not to put glue on the tongues or on the rubber sole. Repeat for the other shoe. Let the glue dry thoroughly. Press down any sticker edges that curl up.

3. Using the sponge brush, apply 3 additional thin layers of glue to each shoe, letting the glue dry thoroughly between each coat.

4. To make 1 shoelace, holding a length of each color ribbon as 1, tie a tight knot ½" from 1 end. (Make sure the knot fits through the lacing holes in the shoe.) Tape the knotted end to a table. Braid the ribbon lengths to within ½" of the remaining end. Tie a tight knot to secure. Repeat with the remaining ribbons for the remaining shoelace. Trim the ends to within ¼" of knot. Apply a small amount of glue to the cut ribbon ends. When the shoelaces and the shoes are thoroughly dry, lace the shoes.

Critter Cloths

Tub time is so much fun when these playful pals help do the scrubbing!

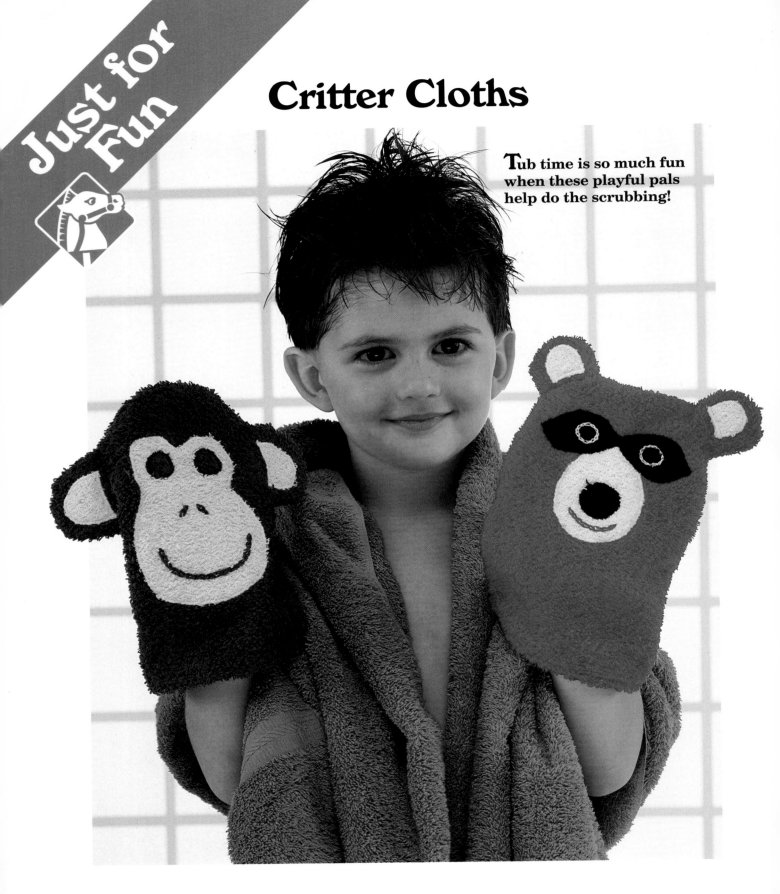

You will need (for each mitt):
Tracing paper
Pencil
Scissors
Paper-backed fusible web
Iron and ironing board
Sewing machine
For the raccoon: ¼ yard red terry cloth, white and black terry cloth scraps, red and white thread, red and white embroidery floss
For the monkey: ¼ yard brown terry cloth, peach terry cloth scraps, brown and peach thread, brown embroidery floss

1. For each, trace the patterns on pages 124 and 125 onto the tracing paper, transferring the details. Cut them out. Fold the ¼ yard of terry cloth in half. Trace the head pattern onto the folded terry cloth. Cut out through both layers.

2. For the monkey: Trace the face, eyes, and both inner ear patterns onto the fusible web. Cut them out. Following the manufacturer's instructions, fuse the face and the inner ears onto a single layer of peach terry cloth; fuse the eyes onto a single layer of brown terry cloth. Cut them out.

3. For the raccoon: Trace the eyes, nose, muzzle, and both inner ear patterns onto the fusible web. Cut them out. Following the manufacturer's instructions, fuse the eyes and the nose to a single layer of black terry cloth; fuse the muzzle and the inner ears to a single layer of white terry cloth. Cut them out.

4. Referring to the photo and the pattern, fuse the pieces in place on 1 head piece. Machine-appliqué, using matching thread and a zigzag stitch.

5. For the monkey: Using the brown embroidery floss, chainstitch the nose and the mouth.

6. For the raccoon: Using the white embroidery floss, chainstitch the eye details. Using the red embroidery floss, chainstitch the mouth.

7. With the raw edges aligned, stack the appliquéd head piece facedown on the remaining head piece. Stitch them together, leaving the bottom edge open. To finish the bottom of the mitt, zigzag along the raw edge. Fold the bottom edge up ½" and hem. Turn.

Monkey

Inner Ear

Eyes

Trace ear; reverse
and trace on
opposite side of
head at dotted line.

Face

Head

124

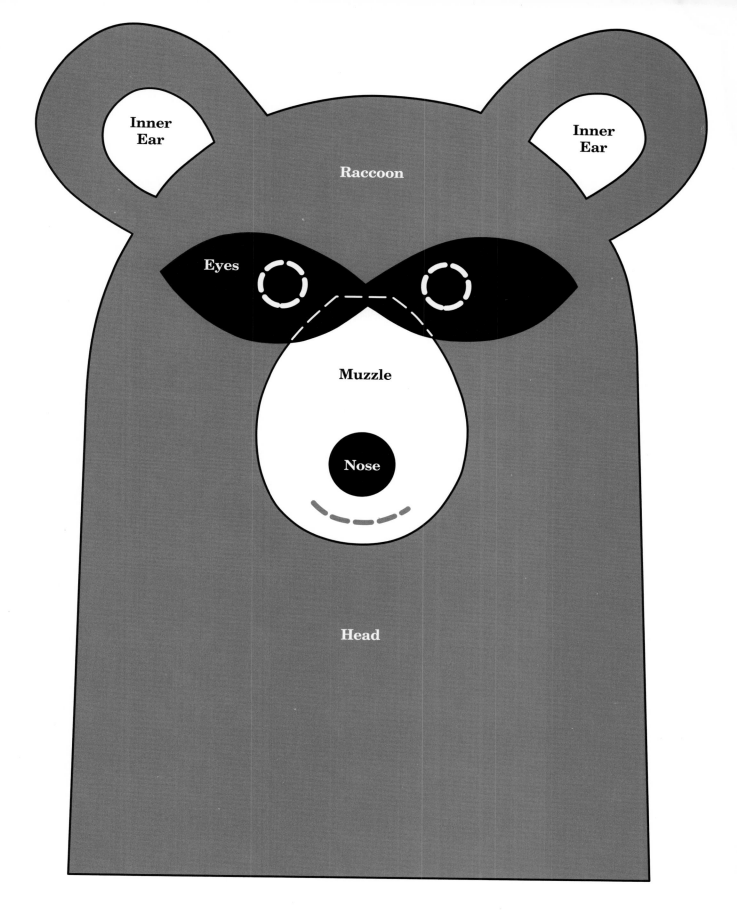

Inner
Ear

Inner
Ear

Raccoon

Eyes

Muzzle

Nose

Head

Too-Easy Toy Net

Rub-a-dub-dub, toys won't clutter the tub with this drip-dry net!

You will need:
5 yards 1"-wide brightly colored double-fold
   bias tape
Pencil
Sewing machine
36"-diameter circle white polyester mesh
Thread to match bias tape
Safety pin
2 (54") lengths ¼"-wide white cording

1. Fold the bias tape in half lengthwise twice. Using a pencil, mark the fold that is opposite the raw ends, making sure to mark the outside and the inside of the fold. Unfold.

2. Unfold the bias tape's center crease. Machine-stitch 1 (1¼"-wide) horizontal buttonhole on each side of each mark, spacing each pair of buttonholes ½" apart. Be sure to make the pairs along the same edge of the bias tape.

3. Encase the raw edge of the mesh circle with the bias tape. Machine-stitch close to the inside edge through all layers.

4. Attach the safety pin to 1 end of 1 length of cording. Thread it through 1 buttonhole into the bias tape casing, returning the cording through the adjacent buttonhole. Tie the cut ends of the cording together. Repeat with the remaining length of cording and the remaining buttonholes.

5. Pull the cording tightly on both sides to close the toy net.

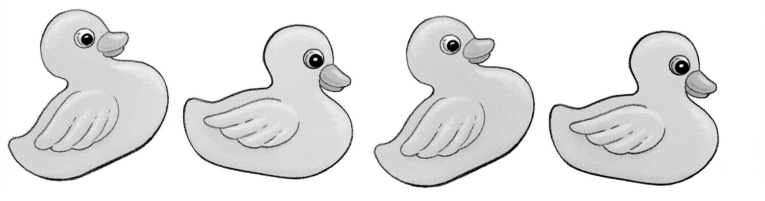

For the Birds

This birdseed-bejeweled cottage is a great natural accent for any child's room.

You will need:
Tracing paper
Pencil
Scissors
Cardboard scraps: 1 (3" x 4¼"), 2 (8" x 16"), 1 (6" x 8¹⁄₁₆"), 1 (1¼" x 3¾"), 1 (1¼" x 1⅝")
Carbon paper
Ruler
Craft knife
Cutting board
Masking tape
Waxed paper
Paintbrushes
Founder's Adhesive glue
Birdseed
3 wooden craft sticks
Acrylic paints: red, brown
Decorator moss

Note: This birdhouse is for inside use only.

1. Trace the front/back and chimney patterns on page 130 onto the tracing paper. Cut them out. Transfer the chimney 2 times onto the 3" x 4¼" scrap of cardboard and the front/back 2 times onto 1 (8" x 16") scrap. Using the carbon paper, transfer the arched opening onto 1 front/back piece. Using the ruler and the pencil, mark a vertical line along the center of the remaining 8" x 16" scrap. Place the cardboard on the cutting board. Using the craft knife, score along the vertical line on the marked 8" x 16" scrap. Cut out the front/back and chimney pieces and the arched opening.

2. Using the masking tape, attach the bottom edge of the front/back pieces to the 8¹⁄₁₆" edges of the 6" x 8¹⁄₁₆" scrap of cardboard so that the three pieces lay flat. Assemble the chimney by taping together the 2 chimney pieces and the 1¼" x 3¾" and 1¼" x 1⅝" scraps to form a box.

3. Cover a table with the waxed paper to protect the surface. Using a paintbrush, apply glue to 1 side of the front/back pieces and to the outside of the chimney. Liberally cover glued areas with birdseed. Gently press the birdseed to secure. Let the glue dry.

4. To make the perch, using a craft knife, cut a 2" length off the end of each wooden craft stick. Set them aside. Then cut 2 (1") lengths from the craft stick scraps. Apply glue to 1 side of the 1" craft stick lengths. Align the 1" craft stick lengths parallel and horizontally. Evenly space the 3 (2") craft stick ends and position them vertically on the glue side of the 1" scraps. Let the glue dry.

5. For the perch support, using a craft knife, trim the remaining craft stick scraps to the same size. Then stack them on top of each other and glue them together. Let the glue dry.

6. Letting the paint dry between colors, paint ¾" of the straight end of the perch brown; paint the remainder red. Place the front/back piece birdseed side down. Glue the perch support just below the straight bottom edge of the arched opening.

7. To create the roof, carefully fold the scored 8" x 16" scrap of cardboard in half. To assemble the house, use masking tape to attach the roof to the 6" x 8¹⁄₁₆" bottom piece at the sides. Glue the roof to the bottom piece. Apply glue to the edges of the front/back pieces. Gently bring them up until they are vertical and touch the roof. (The roof will overhang the front and the back of the house.)

8. Referring to the photo and the pattern, position the chimney on the roof. Glue the

chimney in place. Glue the perch to the
perch support.

9. Cover the roof with glue. Spread the
moss over the glue. Gently press the moss
to secure. Using scissors, trim any excess
moss.

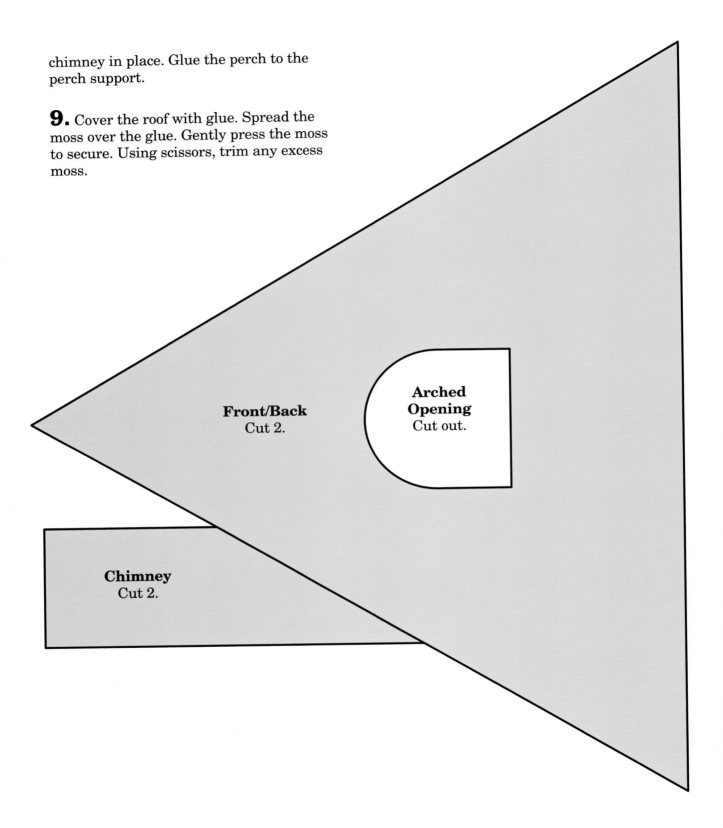

Front/Back
Cut 2.

**Arched
Opening**
Cut out.

Chimney
Cut 2.

Home-Run Curtain Holders

You will need:
Electric drill with ⅛" bit
2 (3½") lengths ⅞"-diameter wooden
   dowel
6 (1"-long) wood screws
2 inside mount shade brackets
Long screwdriver
2 (³⁄₁₆"-diameter) dowel screws
Red spray paint
2 baseballs

1. Drill a hole in each end of 1 wooden
dowel. Slide 1 (1"-long) wood screw through
the center hole of 1 shade bracket. Insert
the screw and the bracket into 1 end of the
dowel. Using the screwdriver, screw them
in place. Screw 1 dowel screw into the
opposite end of the dowel. Repeat for the
second dowel.

2. Spray-paint the dowels and the
brackets. Let the paint dry.

3. Using 2 (1"-long) wood screws for each,
mount the brackets to the window molding
or the wall.

4. Drill a hole into each baseball. Screw 1
baseball onto each dowel.

These easy and inexpensive curtain
holders are sure to be a grand-slam
success with the little leaguer in your
house.

Snow White & Rose Red Sachets

These dolls are more than just pretty faces—their skirts are full of potpourri to sweetly scent your little girl's dresser drawers.

You will need (for each doll):
Fusible interfacing scraps: 1 (5½" x 6"),
    1 (1½" x 3")
2 (5½" x 6") scraps white cotton fabric
Tracing paper
Iron-on transfer pencil
Iron and ironing board
Ultra-fine permanent black marker
#3 and #6 paintbrushes
Brush-on fabric paint dyes: skin tone, pink,
    hair color, eye color, blouse color
Fabric paint dye extender (optional)
Fabric paints with tip: hair color, white
Straight pin
Sewing machine
2 (5½" x 6") scraps thin batting
Thread to match skirt and blouse
Scissors
Pencil
Print fabric scraps for apron: 1 (1½" x 3"),
    1 (6") square
Pinking shears
6" x 14" piece print fabric for skirt
½ cup potpourri
Hot-glue gun with glue sticks
1 (6") length and 1 (11") length ⅜"-wide
    coordinating grosgrain ribbon or 6"
    length ⅜"-wide coordinating rickrack
2 purchased fabric rosettes

1. Following the manufacturer's instructions, with the raw edges aligned, fuse the 5½" x 6" interfacing scrap to the wrong side of 1 (5½" x 6") white fabric scrap.

2. Using the tracing paper and the transfer pencil, trace the front and back patterns on page 135 onto separate sheets of paper, transferring the markings. Center the back facedown on the right side of the interfaced white scrap. Center the front facedown on the right side of the remaining white scrap. Following the manufacturer's instructions, transfer the markings to the fabric scraps, taking care not to shift the paper. Using the permanent marker, trace the transferred markings. Let the markings dry. Rinse the pieces in warm water to remove the pencil markings. Iron dry.

3. Let each color dry before applying the next color. If the fabric soaks up the paint dye too quickly, mix some paint dye extender with the paint dye.

Referring to the patterns and painting approximately ¼" outside the outlines, paint in this order: the face (except the eyes and the lips), the neck, and the hands using the skin tone; the hair using the hair color; the irises using the eye color; the lips and the cheeks using pink; and the blouse using the blouse color. Let the paint dry thoroughly.

4. Using the hair-colored fabric paint, paint the curvy lines in the hair. Using the white fabric paint and the pin, dip the head of the pin into the paint; make a small dot in the right corner of the pupil of each eye. Set aside.

5. Stack 1 (5½" x 6") batting scrap, the back (right side up), and the front (right side down), aligning the markings as closely as possible. Using a ⅛" seam and backstitching at the beginning and the end, stitch the layers together, leaving open where indicated on the pattern. Trim the seam allowances; clip into the corners. Turn and press.

6. Using the pencil, trace the apron and bib patterns onto the tracing paper. Cut them out. With the raw edges aligned, fuse the 1½" x 3" interfacing scrap to the wrong side of the 1½" x 3" apron scrap. Transfer the bib pattern to the fused fabric; transfer the apron pattern to the 6" square of apron fabric. Using pinking shears, cut out the bib and the apron.

7. Run gathering stitches along the top of the apron and along 1 (14") edge of the skirt. With right sides facing, the raw edges aligned, and the short edges together, fold the skirt in half. Using a ¼" seam, stitch along the short edge and the ungathered bottom edge. Turn and press. Insert the remaining batting piece into the skirt. Fill the skirt with the potpourri.

8. Tuck the upper half of the doll into the skirt. Pull the gathering threads so that the skirt fits snugly around the waist. Tie off and trim the threads. Using the hot-glue gun, glue the skirt to the doll in the front and the back.

9. Gather the apron. Tie off and trim the threads. Glue the apron to the center front at the waist. Glue the bib to the center front, overlapping the apron.

10. Glue the 6" length of ribbon or rickrack around the waist, covering the raw edges of the skirt and the apron. Trim the excess. If using the ribbon, tie the 11" length into a bow; glue it to the center back at the waist. Glue the rosettes to the waist and the hair. Let the glue dry thoroughly.

Bib
Cut 1.

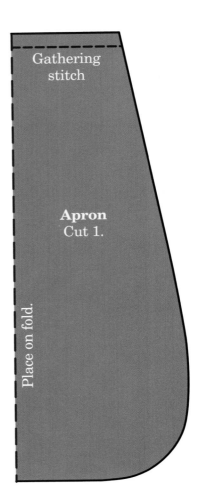

Gathering stitch

Apron
Cut 1.

Place on fold.

Leave open.

Doll Front

Leave open.

Doll Back

Safari Stick Horse

Whether trekking across Africa or the backyard, this zebra is sure to add adventure to an ordinary afternoon. And the rubber ball on the end prevents indoor journeys from scratching the floor.

You will need:
Tracing paper
Pencil
Scissors
Masking tape
12" x 18" pieces Fun Foam: 1 black, 2 white
Thick craft glue
White gloss spray paint
48" length 1"-diameter wooden dowel
Knife
3" to 4"-diameter red rubber ball
Hot-glue gun and glue sticks
2 (½") wiggle eyes
20" length ¾"-wide red ribbon
20" length ¼"-wide purple ribbon
4 (1" to 1½") decorative plastic or metal
   medallions

1. Trace the pattern pieces and the details on pages 138 and 139 onto the tracing paper. Cut them out. (Be sure to cut 2 of each, except the mane.) Using the masking tape, attach the mane, stripes, eyes, and nostril pattern pieces to the black foam; attach the head and neck pattern pieces to the white foam. Cut them out. To make the fringe on the mane, cut along 1 long edge to within ¾" of the opposite edge.

2. Referring to the photo and the pattern, glue the nonfringed edge of the mane in place on 1 head/neck piece. Then apply glue to the wrong side of the head/neck piece along the outer edges. Aligning the edges, glue the head/neck pieces together, leaving the bottom edge open. Glue the stripes in place on both sides of the head/neck. Glue the stripes, the eyes, and the nostrils to both head/ear pieces. Glue the head/ear pieces in place on the head/neck. **Do not** glue the ears to the mane. Let the glue dry thoroughly.

3. Spray-paint the dowel white. Use a knife to cut a 1"-diameter hole in the rubber ball deep enough for the dowel to slide into.

4. Apply hot glue to 1 end of the dowel. Insert the glued end into the zebra as far as possible. Put hot glue into the hole in the ball and stick the ball onto the bottom end of the dowel. Hot-glue the wiggle eyes in place. Let the glue dry.

5. Cut 2 (4") lengths and 2 (6") lengths each from the red ribbon and the purple ribbon. Center and hot-glue the purple ribbon lengths on the corresponding red ribbon lengths. Referring to the photo and the pattern, glue the ribbon sets to the zebra head to create the bridle. Glue the medallions over the ribbon ends.

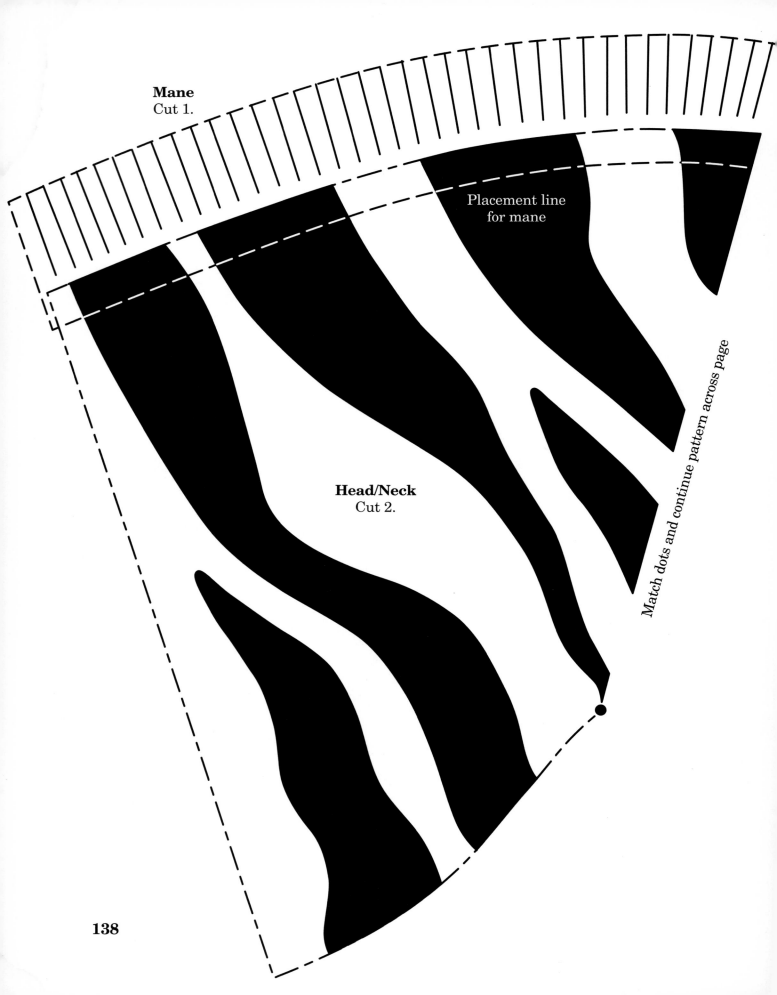

Mane
Cut 1.

Placement line
for mane

Head/Neck
Cut 2.

Match dots and continue pattern across page

138

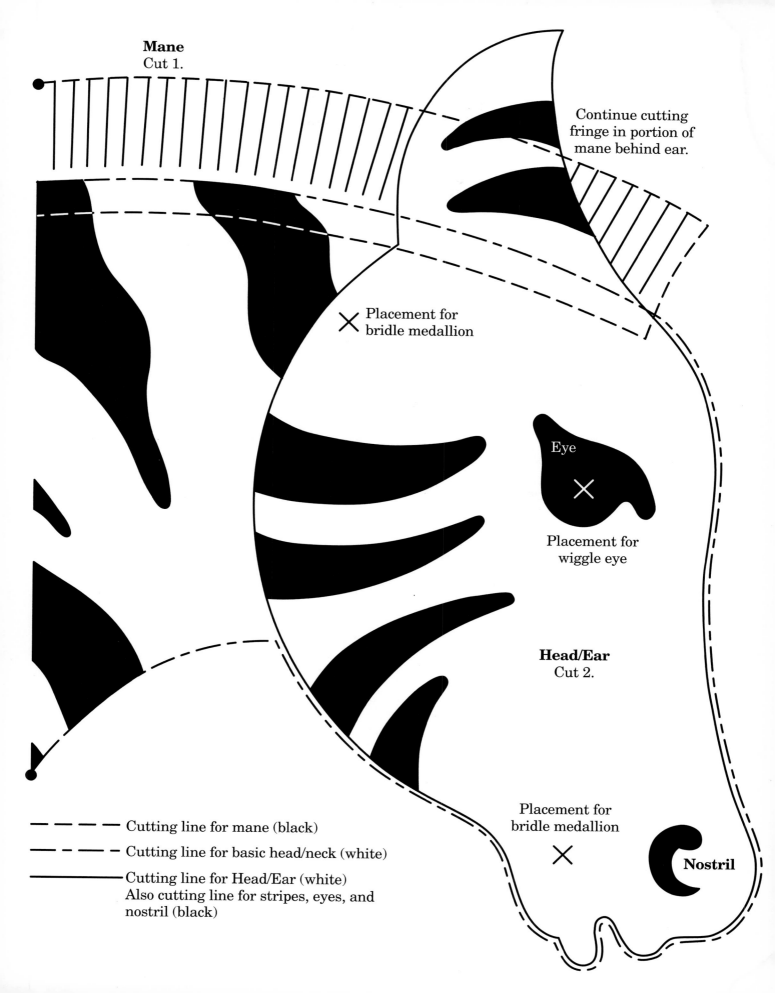

Mane
Cut 1.

Continue cutting
fringe in portion of
mane behind ear.

✕ Placement for
bridle medallion

Eye
✕
Placement for
wiggle eye

Head/Ear
Cut 2.

Placement for
bridle medallion

✕

Nostril

– – – – – Cutting line for mane (black)

– ·· – ·· – Cutting line for basic head/neck (white)

————— Cutting line for Head/Ear (white)
Also cutting line for stripes, eyes, and
nostril (black)

Gear Up for Adventure

Regardless of the direction your little travelers want to head, these bags will get them there in style.

You will need (for all):
Pencil
Tracing paper
Scissors
1 yard paper-backed fusible web
Cotton fabric scraps in desired colors
Iron and ironing board
Purchased garment bag, tote bag, and
　toiletry bag
Fabric paints in desired colors
Plastic garbage bag
Thread to match selected luggage tag
　fabric
3 star buttons

Note: You may need to adjust the sizes of
the embellishments or their placement
depending upon the sizes of the purchased
bags.

1. Determine the desired number and the
placement of the shapes. Trace the arrows
(except the luggage tag pattern), star, and
circle patterns on pages 142 and 143 onto
the tracing paper. Cut them out. Transfer
the patterns onto the fusible web as many
times as desired. Cut them out.

2. Following the manufacturer's
directions, fuse the web shapes onto the
desired color fabrics. Cut them out.

3. Fuse the shapes in the desired positions
on each bag.

4. Using the fabric paints, outline the
shapes to seal the fabric edges. Add dot and
squiggle embellishments if desired.

5. **For each luggage tag:** Trace the
luggage tag pattern onto tracing paper. Cut
it out. Transfer 2 tag shapes onto the
desired color fabric and 1 tag shape onto
the fusible web. Cut them out. Following
the manufacturer's directions, fuse the 2
fabric layers together, with the wrong sides
together.

　Cover a table with the plastic bag to
protect the surface. Using the paint pens,
outline 1 side of the tag. Write the child's
name on the tag. Include the address and
the phone number if desired. Let the paint
dry. Turn the tag over and outline the
opposite side. Let the paint dry. Wrap the
tag around 1 bag handle and sew the tag
layers together. Secure with a button.

Cut here for short arrow.

142